THE LAST DIARY OF TSARITSA ALEXANDRA

The Last Diary of Tsaritsa Alexandra

Introduction by
Robert K. Massie

Edited by
Vladimir A. Kozlov and Vladimir M. Khrustalëv

Notes edited by
Alexandra Raskina

Notes, chronology, glossary, and afterword translated by Laura E. Wolfson

Preparation of the diary, notes, and appendixes supervised by Timothy D. Sergay

Yale University Press
New Haven and London

Published with the cooperation of the State Archive of the Russian Federation.

Published with assistance from the William T. Morris Foundation.

Frontispiece: The 1918 diary of Tsaritsa Alexandra.

Designed by James J. Johnson, and set in Sabon Roman type by The Composing Room of Michigan, Inc. Printed in the United States of America by Vail-Ballou Press, Binghamton, New York.

Library of Congress Cataloging-in-Publication Data

Alexandra, Empress, consort of Nicholas II, Emperor of Russia, 1872–1918.
The last diary of Tsaritsa Alexandra / edited by Vladimir A. Kozlov and Vladimir M. Khrustalëv ; introduction by Robert K. Massie.
p. cm.
Includes bibliographical references.
ISBN 0-300-07212-0 (cl. : alk. paper)

1. Alexandra, Empress, consort of Nicholas II, Emperor of Russia, 1872–1918—Diaries. 2. Alexandra, Empress, consort of Nicholas II, Emperor of Russia, 1872–1918—Last years. 3. Empresses—Russia—Diaries. 4. Russia—History—Nicholas II, 1894–1917. 5. Soviet Union—History—Revolution, 1917–1921. I. Kozlov, V. A. (Vladimir Aleksandrovich) II. Khrustalëv, Vladimir M. III. Title.
DK254.A5A3 1997
947.08'3'092—dc21
[B] 97-15675

A catalogue record for this book is available from the British Library.

The paper in this book meets the guidelines for permanence and durability of the Committee on Production Guidelines for Book Longevity of the Council on Library Resources.

10 9 8 7 6 5 4 3 2 1

Contents

Introduction

Robert K. Massie

On a morning in July 1907, a young woman, recently engaged to an officer on the Russian imperial yacht, waited to be introduced to the Empress (or Tsaritsa) Alexandra, the thirty-five-year-old consort of Emperor (or Tsar) Nicholas II. The meeting was to take place in a tropical greenhouse at Peterhof, the imperial park on the Gulf of Finland. Eventually, the empress appeared. "Advancing through the masses of greenery, came a tall and slender figure," Lili Dehn remembered many years later. "[She] was dressed entirely in white with a thin white veil draped around her hat. Her complexion was delicately fair . . . her hair was reddish gold, her eyes were dark blue. . . . I remember that her pearls were magnificent and that diamond earrings flashed colored fires whenever she moved her head. . . . I noticed that she spoke Russian with a strong English accent."[1]

Ten years later, Tsaritsa Alexandra, her husband, and their five children were prisoners in another palace; eleven years later, on the night of 16–17 July 1918, they were murdered in a Siberian cellar.

When the downfall came, a torrent of calumny poured on Alexandra's head. During the war with Germany she was called "the German woman," a German spy, a traitor to Russia. In fact, Alexandra despised Imperial Germany and its strutting monarch, Kaiser Wilhelm II. Her own small grand-duchy of Hesse-Darmstadt had entered the new empire hostile to the dominance of Prussia and the Hohenzollern dynasty and, throughout her life, Alexandra thought of herself as Hessian, not German. She blamed the outbreak of the First World War on the "idiotic pride and insatiable ambition of the Hohenzollerns," and bluntly declared, "Prussia has meant Germany's ruin." In fact, Alexandra's childhood surroundings, education, appearance, personal habits, beliefs, and moral outlook were almost entirely drawn from the tradition and culture of England, not of Germany. When she married the Tsar of Russia, she became, in certain respects, extravagantly Russian. But Pierre Gilliard, a Swiss tutor who spent thirteen years at the Russian court, never heard the empress speak German.

Alexandra was also accused, before and after the Revolution, of having been the mistress of Grigory Rasputin, the flamboyant Siberian "holy man" whose sexual antics were the subject of leering discussion by every literate person in Russia—except the empress. This was as untrue as the accusation of treason. Alexandra believed in Rasputin because he presented himself as a messenger from God and a true representative of the Russian peasantry and because he seemed to be the only person able to preserve the life of her hemophiliac son, the tsarevich Alexis. His claims on the first two counts were fraudulent; her belief that he could save her son, however, was supported by the evidence of numerous occasions when he seemed to have done precisely that.

After Alexandra's death, 630 letters written to her husband were found in a black leather suitcase in Ekaterinburg; of these, 230 were written over the period from the couple's first meeting to the outbreak of war in 1914; the other 400 were written during the war years, 1914–1917. She wrote, pouring out a cataract of thoughts and emotions, never imagining that any eyes but his would read her words. Once published, these letters immediately became key historical documents, helping to explain events, personalities, and decisions at the summit of the autocracy on the eve of the Russian Revolution.

The demise of the Soviet state has made available other

documents long secluded in Moscow archives. Among them are Alexandra's diaries for the years 1887–1892, 1894, and 1916–1918. The current volume, covering 1918, was presented to her on 1 January by her second daughter, Tatiana, and records the final six and a half months of her life. Its cryptic, unemotional style stands in sharp contrast to the tumultuous style of her letters. Here she is creating, for herself alone, a simple record of the highlights of each day: the weather and temperature; family illnesses and health; meals; periods and subjects of study; visitors (welcome and unwelcome); books read; games played. Her religious faith is evident. On the diary's first page, she displays her effort to master the numerical system of Old Church Slavonic (different from everyday Russian, which uses Arabic numerals). Through the diary, she records saint's days, feast days, and other religious holidays. Every religious service held by the family in Tobolsk and Ekaterinburg is set down. Usually, her feelings about an event break through only in a highly abbreviated form. Nevertheless, despite its style and brevity, the diary is filled with poignancy and drama. Alexandra does not know what is going to happen; the modern reader does. Fleshed out by our knowledge from other sources, this diary gives a clear picture of these grim weeks and tells us much about the character of this much-criticized, reclusive, and melancholy woman.

Alix Victoria Helena Louise Beatrice, princess of Hesse-Darmstadt, was born on 6 June 1872 in that small grand duchy of the newly created German Empire. Named Alix after her mother, Princess Alice of England, the third of Queen Victoria's nine children, she was "a sweet, merry little person, always laughing and a dimple in one cheek," as her mother wrote to her august grandmother. In infancy, she was given the nickname "Sunny." On marrying Grand Duke Louis of Hesse, Princess Alice had transformed his small palace and household into England in miniature. The drawing rooms were hung with portraits of Queen Victoria, Prince Albert, and the English cousins. Sketches of English palaces and English scenes adorned the bedchambers. An English governess, Mary Anne Orchard, ruled the nursery, administering a rigid schedule with fixed hours for every activity. Meals were simple: dessert consisted of baked apples or rice pudding, except on Christmas, when dinner concluded with plum pudding and mince pies imported from England. Every summer, the Hessian children visited England and stayed with "Granny" at Windsor Castle, at Balmoral in the Highlands, or at Osborne House on the Isle of Wight.

In 1878, when Alix was six, diphtheria carried away her mother and her younger sister. As a precaution against the disease, all of Alix's dolls and toys were burned. Desolate, the little girl began to seal herself off, building a shell of aloofness which only a few would penetrate. Queen Victoria attempted to keep watch over this small granddaughter as best she could; tutors and governesses in Darmstadt were required to send special reports to Windsor and received in return a steady flow of instruction from the queen. Alix was a good student. She acquired a grounding in European history and geography; she became bilingual in English and German, and she also spoke French. She played the piano with amateur brilliance but disliked playing in front of people. When Queen Victoria asked her to play for guests at Windsor, Alix obliged, but a flush across her face and shoulders betrayed her torment. As the years in Darmstadt and England went by, her upbringing was thoroughly English and entirely Victorian. The future empress of Russia was molded into a proper English gentlewoman.

The youngest of four living sisters, Alix watched her sisters marry. Victoria, the eldest, chose a titled but impoverished German-born British naval officer, Prince Louis of Battenberg, who became First Sea Lord of the Royal Navy at the outbreak of the First World War. Alix's sister Irene married a German, Prince Heinrich of Prussia, the only brother of Kaiser Wilhelm II. Her sister Elizabeth, called Ella, married the Russian Grand Duke Sergei Alexandrovich, a younger brother of Russian Emperor Alexander III. Eventually, Alix, the shy, youngest sister, outshone them all by marrying Alexander III's son, Nicholas II, and herself becoming empress of Russia.

Alix met Nicholas at Ella and Sergei's wedding in St. Petersburg in 1884, when Alix was twelve and Nicholas was sixteen. They met again five years later, and although there was an attraction on this occasion, they were not engaged until 1894. They were married suddenly that year when Tsar Alexander III unexpectedly died of nephritis, and his brothers, the uncles of the new tsar, decided that the untried twenty-six-year-old Nicholas needed the steadying influence of marriage. For his new twenty-two-year-old wife, the sequence was bewildering: overnight, it seemed, she converted from Lutheranism to Orthodoxy, her name was changed from Alix to Alexandra, and she was married.

The marriage was a life-long success. "How contented and happy I am with my beloved Nicky," she wrote to one of her sisters during her first weeks in St. Petersburg. She had a husband who, she knew, loved and relied upon her absolutely. Over the years, this reliance was to give Alexandra enormous influence over Nicholas. She had come to him at a moment of overpowering crisis. "I am not prepared to be a tsar. I never wanted to become one. I know nothing of the business of ruling," he had confessed to a cousin when he mounted the throne. Thereafter, Alexandra gave him the confidence that no one else—not his mother, his uncles, his brothers and sisters, his cousins, nor his ministers—was able to provide.

In contrast to the private success of her marriage, the public appearance of the new empress in St. Petersburg was an immediate failure. "I feel myself completely alone. I weep and worry all day long because I feel that my husband is so young and so inexperienced," she wrote to a friend in Germany. The first ceremonial exposures of the reserved young woman from a small, provincial court on the Rhine were blighted by shyness and fright. As she stood beside her husband, people filing past in reception lines found themselves confronting a tall, cold-eyed figure, silent and unsmiling, her hand rigidly extended for a perfunctory kiss. Alexandra, in turn, quickly decided that the moral life of the capital, including that of many members of her own husband's family, was idle, listless, and decadent. Scandalized by the profusion of flaunted love affairs among the aristocracy, she began reviewing palace invitation lists and crossing off names. Society, in a cycle of mutual dislike and rebuff, disdainfully pronounced the young empress a prude and a bore. Alexandra withdrew further into her shell.

Pleading headaches, backaches, and pregnancy (she gave birth five times during her first ten years of marriage), she relinquished all but the most essential contact with Russian society.

A place of shelter in this storm was Alexandra's fervent new attachment to the Orthodox church. She had not given up her devout Lutheranism easily; for months before her marriage, the requirement that a prospective Russian empress convert to Orthodoxy had been the chief impediment to her acceptance of Nicholas. Repeatedly, he had tried to persuade her; for days, she had wept and whispered, "No, I cannot." Nicholas was determined and, eventually, she capitulated. "We were left alone and with her first words she consented. . . . I cried like a child and she did too," he wrote to his mother.

Alexandra embraced her new religion with passionate intensity. In Russia, she assumed that she would find among both aristocrats and peasants a closely knit community of devout believers. Her discovery that many Russians had little use for this kind of religion shocked the young empress; her reaction, again, was to withdraw. Her place, she concluded, was with the church in its purest, most zealous, and, some said, most primitive form. She went to church every day. She read constantly from the Bible and the lives of the saints. She collected rare icons and, believing that healing power emanated from these works of art, arranged them carefully in rooms she occupied. Certain Russians of that day dabbled in mysticism, spiritualism, and the occult. Alexandra refused to rule out the possibility that these might be legitimate approaches to God. She made religious pilgrimages and looked forward to conversations with religious hermits, mystics, "soul doctors," and peasant holy men.

Alexandra's other place of refuge was her family. From the beginning, she and Nicholas hoped for a son, as, since the reign of Emperor Paul at the beginning of the nineteenth century, only males could succeed to the Russian throne. Their first four children were daughters—Olga, Tatiana, Marie, and Anastasia. Their fifth child, born 12 August 1904, was the long-desired boy, a blue-eyed, golden-haired infant christened Alexis. He was, according to the Swiss tutor Pierre Gilliard, "the center of this united family. . . . His sisters worshipped him. He was his parents' pride and joy. When he was well, the palace was transformed. Everyone and everything in it seemed bathed in sunshine."[2] But Alexis was a hemophiliac. This disease, which appears only in males and is transmitted by hereditary laws from mother to son, is characterized by the inability of blood to clot normally. In Alexis's case, it was handed down to him by the first royal hemophilic carrier, his great-grandmother Queen Victoria. The queen's fourth son, Prince Leopold, was a hemophiliac, and at least two of her daughters and three of her granddaughters were carriers. One of these granddaughters was Alexandra.

The blow further altered Alexandra's life. When the tsarevich was born, there was little that medicine or science could do to halt the flow of blood from a ruptured internal blood vessel. Minor external cuts and scratches were not dangerous—they could be treated by pressure and tight bandaging—but internal bleeding, particularly into the confined space of a knee, ankle, or elbow joint, meant excruciating pain and crippling. Blood seeping into surrounding tissue and muscle could create a hematoma as large as a grapefruit which pressed inward on the nerves. The pain brought screams and groans and, eventually, exhaustion when Alexis, white-faced, lying in bed with his head resting on his mother's arm, could only look up and whisper, "Mummy." Alexandra could do nothing except hold his hand and kiss his forehead.

Throughout Alexis's life, his health was Alexandra's principal preoccupation. Talk of his condition dominates her letters to her husband and the pages of her diary. Year after year, specialists were consulted and shook their heads. Because the normal world was powerless, Alexandra drew up other battle plans. Her family was a place where sadness need not be hidden nor pretense offered. She sought answers from her new church, which teaches its believers that suffering is an experience that enriches the soul. Through the vigor and frequency of her prayers, she determined to wrest from God the miracle that science denied. "God is just," she declared and begged for mercy for her son. When Alexis was well, she dared to hope. Even as the years passed and one hemorrhage followed another, she refused to believe that God had deserted her. Knowing that the disease had been transmitted through her own body, she fixed on her own unworthiness. If she was the instrument of her son's torture, she could not also be the instrument of his salvation. She must, therefore, find someone closer to God who would intercede on her behalf. When Rasputin, the Siberian peasant reported to possess miraculous powers of faith healing, arrived in St. Petersburg, Alexandra believed that her prayers had been answered.

Incredibly, as this desperate, personal battle was being waged, Russia did not know. Afraid to inform the nation that the heir to the throne lived under the constant shadow of death, the few who knew connived to erect a façade of normalcy. In film footage of public appearances of the imperial family, Alexis is often carried in the arms of a husky sailor. Today, no one notices; then, those who noticed did not ask why. The secret was kept. Even the Swiss tutor Pierre Gilliard, who came to the palace five times a week to tutor the children in French, did not know. Whenever his youngest pupil disappeared, his four young female students became melancholy and distracted. But when he asked the reason, the boy's sisters answered evasively, "Alexis Nicholaievich is not well."[3]

Because the condition of the tsarevich was never revealed, Russians were unable to accurately judge the character of the empress or the true nature of her relationship with Rasputin. Unaware of her ordeal, they ascribed her remoteness and the look of permanent sadness on her face to hostility toward Russia. As she devoted herself to lengthening hours of prayer, her own public appearances were further curtailed. When she did emerge, she was more silent, colder, and more withdrawn. During wartime, with Russian anger inflamed against Germany, the various complaints Russians had against the empress—her German birth, her aloofness, her devotion to Rasputin—merged into a sweeping torrent of suspicion and wrath.

Despite her conversion to Orthodoxy and embrace of Russian culture, England remained a vital part of Alexandra's life. Although she knew French and German and eventually achieved fluency in Russian, her everyday language was English. She and Nicholas normally spoke and wrote to each other in English. She spoke English to her daughters and wrote in English to her sisters. Nicholas conversed with his children in Russian, although, in the evening, he often read aloud to them from French and English novels, as well as Russian classics. In captivity, Alexandra began to teach her older daughters German.

Alexandra's English practicality was displayed in the orderly daily routines by which her Russian family lived. This regimented schedule stemmed not only from Alexandra's memories of Mrs. Orchard's Darmstadt routine, but from Mrs. Orchard herself, who had followed the empress to Russia and taken charge of the Russian imperial nursery. The empress's work habits always seemed more English than Russian, more Protestant than Orthodox. She preached that life is meant for work, not pleasure, and she insisted that her daughters plunge themselves into learning, correspondence, charitable work, or, failing all else when their hands were idle, needlework and embroidery.

Physically, Alexandra could not always follow her own prescriptions. "She keeps to her bed most of the day, does not receive anyone, does not come out to lunches and remains on the balcony day after day," Nicholas wrote to his mother, the dowager empress Marie. Neither Alexandra nor her doctors could pinpoint the medical cause. As a girl, she had suffered from sciatica, a severe pain in the back and legs, and this scourge reappeared throughout her life. Her pregnancies—four in the first six years of marriage—were difficult. The battle against her son's hemophilia left her physically and emotionally drained. At times of crisis, she sat without relief beside Alexis's bed; once the danger had passed, she collapsed, sometimes for weeks, moving about only by wheelchair. In 1908, when the tsarevich was four, she developed a condition which she referred to as an "enlarged heart." No one doubted that something was wrong. "Her breath came in quick, obviously painful gasps. I often saw her lips turn blue," said the tsar's sister, Grand Duchess Olga.[4] Dr. Yevgeny Botkin, the family physician, came to the palace every day at nine and again at five to listen to her heart. He noted, interestingly, that when the empress was among people she liked and trusted, her heart trouble did not assert itself. But if a situation developed contrary to her liking, or if something was said or done against her wishes, she immediately began to complain about her heart. Years later, in Siberia, Botkin mentioned that he believed his patient suffered from "progressive hysteria."[5] In modern medical terminology, the empress undoubtedly was suffering from psychosomatic symptoms brought on by anxiety—including, most prominently, her worry over the health of her son.

Despite her infirmities, Alexandra's romantic passion for her husband never waned. After twenty years of marriage, the empress, who was shy and reserved about expressing emotion in public, still poured out her feelings in her letters. She began, "Good morning, my darling . . . My beloved one . . . My sweetest treasure . . . My own beloved angel." She concluded: "Sleep well, my treasure . . . I yearn to hold you in my arms and rest my head upon your shoulder." During the war, when Nicholas left for the front, Alexandra wrote, "Oh, my love! It was hard bidding you goodbye and seeing that lonely pale face with big sad eyes . . . my heart cried out, take me with you. . . . I longed to have you near me . . . [to] bend over you, bless you, and gently kiss your sweet face all over—oh my darling, how intensely dear you are to me!" Never imagining that anyone else would read her letters, she reminded him of the childish, sentimental names they had for each other's genitalia. Nicholas's replies were more restrained, but no less tender. "My beloved Sunny, when I read your letters my eyes are moist . . . I don't know how I could have endured it all if God had not decreed to give you to me as a wife and friend. I speak in earnest. At times it is difficult to speak of such things and it is easier for me to put it down on paper, owing to stupid shyness . . . Goodbye, my beloved sweet Sunny."

As the threat of war spread across Europe in July 1914, Alexandra pleaded with her husband to hold Russia aloof. She brandished a telegram from Rasputin in Siberia, opposing the war and predicting that, if war came, it would mean the destruction of the Romanov dynasty and empire. Nicholas brushed the telegram aside; at that stage, his indulgence of Rasputin's connection with his family did not include intrusion into state affairs. When the tsar ordered general mobilization of the Russian army in response to the Austrian bombardment of Belgrade, Alexandra declared, "It's not true." Hurrying to her husband's study, she argued frantically with him for half an hour. Then, returning to her room, she dropped on a couch and murmured, "War! And I knew nothing of it. This is the end of everything."[6]

Ironically, the coming of the war transformed the empress. Alexandra always seemed happiest when immersed in other people's problems, and war gave almost endless scope to this side of her nature. Burning with patriotic enthusiasm, she put aside her own illnesses and plunged into hospital work. "To some it may seem unnecessary my doing this," she said, "but help is much needed and my hand is useful." The huge, ornate Catherine Palace at Tsarskoe Selo, used for receptions and balls before the war, was converted into a military hospital, and before the end of 1914 eighty-five hospitals were operating under her patronage in the Petrograd area alone. In this work, Alexandra did not become simply an imperial patron. She enrolled herself and her two older daughters in a nurses' training course, and every morning at nine, dressed in the gray uniforms of nursing sisters, they left the palace for the hospital. The atmosphere in this place was shocking and brutal. Every day, Red Cross trains brought wounded and dying men—dirty, bloodstained, feverish, and groaning—from the front. The empress and her daughters cleaned and bandaged these mangled bodies. "I have seen the Empress of Russia in the operating room," said her friend Anna Vyrubova, "holding ether cones, handling sterilized instruments, taking from the hands of busy surgeons amputated legs and arms, removing bloody and vermin-ridden field dressings."[7]

It was horror, but it was also fulfillment. Alexandra was drawn to nursing not only by her Victorian work ethic, but also by her familiarity with suffering. Sensitized by her son's hemophilia and by her own ill health, she identified with people in pain. "I never saw her happier than on the day, at the end of her two months' training, she marched at the head of the procession of nurses to receive the Red Cross diploma of a certified war nurse," Vyrubova continued. To Alexandra, these men were Russia itself, bleeding and dying. And she—kneeling beside them to pray, holding their hands when they died—was the Russian empress, *Matushka,* the mother of all the brave men and boys who were giving themselves for the motherland.

Alexandra's devotion to her hospitals did not fail, but eventually her energy and health gave way. This did not stop her pen. Lying on a chaise longue in her mauve boudoir under portraits of the Virgin Mary and Marie Antoinette, or sitting on her balcony looking out at the park with a writing tablet on her knees, she wrote voluminously. She began early in the morning, added paragraphs during the day, went on for pages late at night, and perhaps added more the following day. She wrote mostly in English, in torrential, breathless prose with irregular spelling, many abbreviations, frequent omissions of words that seemed obvious, and punctuation made up largely of dots and dashes.

During the war, writing to Nicholas, she applied this prose style to extended political exhortation. Worried about the future of Russia, her family, and the inheritance awaiting her son, Alexandra attempted to influence her husband's passive, almost mystical, resignation to fate. Throughout his life, Nicholas had tried to do what he thought was right; when the result was failure, he tended to accept what had happened as the will of God. Alexandra's concept of suffering was different: Suffering was a part of life. Sometimes it was ennobling, but unless it came unmistakably from God, it need not be passively accepted. In the political arena, she insisted, it was often one's duty to stand up and fight. In particular, she believed that the tsar had an imperative responsibility to do whatever was necessary to preserve the autocracy. "On the day of my coronation," Nicholas had said, "I swore to preserve the autocracy and shoulder the whole burden of governing my people. I must keep that oath intact for my son." In upholding this oath, Alexandra believed, irresolution and fatalism could lead to catastrophe. As she saw it, her own sacred duty was to prevent this from happening.

"Forgive me, my precious one," she wrote in 1915, "but you know you are too kind and gentle—sometimes a good loud voice can do wonders and a severe look—do, my love, be more decided and sure of yourself. . . . Humility is God's greatest gift but a sovereign needs to show his will more often." Repeatedly, her letters inveighed against the demand of the Duma, or representative body, for greater participation in government: "We are not a constitutional country and dare not be, our people are not educated for it. . . . Never forget that you are and must remain autocratic emperor. . . . For Baby's sake we must be firm as otherwise his inheritance will be awful, as with his character he won't bow down to others but be his own master, as one must in Russia whilst people are so uneducated." A year later, shortly before Nicholas's abdication, a torrent of political advice poured from Alexandra's pen: "I am fully convinced that great and beautiful times are coming for your reign and Russia . . . we must give a strong country to Baby and dare not be weak for his sake, else he will have a harder reign, setting our faults right and drawing the reins in tightly which you let loose. . . . He has a strong will and mind of his own, don't let things slip through your fingers and make him build all over again. Be firm . . . one wants to feel your hand—how long, years, people have told me the same, 'Russia loves to feel the whip'—it's their nature—tender love and then the iron hand to punish and guide. How I wish I could pour my will into your veins. . . . Be Peter the Great, Ivan the Terrible, Emperor Paul—crush them all under you—now don't you laugh, naughty one."

Nicholas replied, figuratively shaking his head: "My dear, tender thanks for the severe scolding. I read it with a smile because you speak to me as though I was a child . . . Your 'poor little weak-willed' hubby, Nicky."

On 15 March 1917, confronted by revolution in the capital and the unanimous recommendation of all Russian generals that he step aside, Nicholas II abdicated the throne he had occupied for twenty-three years. His decision, effected in Pskov, 160 miles south of Petrograd, occurred without the knowledge of the empress, who was at Tsarskoe Selo, preoccupied with an outbreak of measles which had placed all but one of her children in darkened rooms with high fever. The palace lay naked to the mob; Nicholas's cousin, Grand Duke

Kirill, who hated the imperial couple, had withdrawn a protecting battalion of the elite Guarde Equipage. The following day, Kirill led his men down the Nevsky Prospect and offered his services to the revolution. Then he went home and raised a red flag over his palace.

Alexandra learned about the abdication on the evening of the sixteenth. "The door opened and the empress appeared," recalled Lili Dehn. "Her face was distorted with agony, her eyes were full of tears. She tottered rather than walked. . . . Taking my hands in hers, she said brokenly, '*Abdiqué!*' . . . I waited for her next words. . . . 'The poor dear . . . all alone down there . . . what he has gone through, oh my God, what he has gone through. . . . And I was not there to console him.'"[8]

Six days later, the former tsar, now titled "Citizen Romanov," returned home. For the next four months, he and his family were held prisoners in the Alexander Palace at Tsarskoe Selo. In the light of their later experience, the regime was not strict: the family remained in its own surroundings, waited on by its own servants, dining off its own plates. But they were no longer free to go where they wanted or see whom they wished. Bands of soldiers roamed the corridors, bawling, "Where is The Heir?" "Show us The Heir!" Excursions were confined to limited areas of the imperial park where they were permitted to walk, row on the lake, and plant a vegetable garden. They endured rudeness and occasional humiliation: a toy rifle was wrenched from Alexis's hands by a soldier; another guard amused himself by poking a bayonet between the spokes of Nicholas's bicycle, sending the former monarch sprawling.

The Romanovs' principal jailer was Alexander Kerensky, Minister of Justice in the Provisional Government formed by members of the Duma after Nicholas's abdication. On 3 April, Kerensky arrived to inspect his prisoners. The minister later admitted that his manner had been abrupt and nervous:

> To be frank I was anything but calm before this first meeting with Nicholas II. . . . All the way along the endless chain of official apartments, I was struggling for control of my emotions. . . . The imperial family were standing near the window. . . . From this cluster . . . there stepped out somewhat

> hesitantly a man of medium height in a military kit who walked forward to meet me with a slight peculiar smile. It was the emperor. . . . He stopped in confusion. He did not know what to do . . . I hurriedly walked over . . . shook hands and sharply said, "Kerensky" as I always do. Nicholas II gave my hand a firm grasp, immediately recovering from his confusion, and smiling . . . led me to his family. His daughters and the Heir Apparent were obviously burning with curiosity and their eyes were simply glued to me. But Alexandra Feodorovna stood tense and erect—proud, domineering, irreconcilable; she held out her hand to me, slowly and unwillingly.[9]

Not long after, Kerensky returned to the palace to conduct an investigation of the empress's "treasonable, pro-German" activities. This interview was casual, lasting only an hour. The minister began by politely and mildly asking about the role she had played in politics. She replied that she and the tsar were "the most united of couples, whose whole joy and pleasure was in their family life, and that they had no secrets from each other; that they discussed everything, and that it was not surprising that in the last years which had been so troubled, they had often discussed politics. . . . It was true that they had discussed the different appointments of ministers, but this could not be otherwise in a marriage such as theirs." Kerensky was "struck by the clarity, the energy, and the frankness of her words," and reported to his governmental colleagues that Alexandra had been loyal to Russia. He requested that the Petrograd newspapers, which had been virulently attacking the Romanovs, "put an end to their campaign against the tsar and more particularly the empress."

Kerensky's impressions of the imperial couple, particularly of Nicholas, continued to improve. Kerensky himself reported that he was affected by Nicholas's "unassuming manner and complete absence of pose. Perhaps it was this natural, quite artless simplicity that gave the Emperor that peculiar fascination, that charm which was further increased by his wonderful eyes, deep and sorrowful. . . . It cannot be said that my talks with the tsar were due to a special desire on his part; he was obliged to see me . . . yet the former emperor never once lost his equilibrium; never failed to act as a courteous man of the world."

From its beginnings, the authority of the Provisional Government was challenged by the Petrograd Soviet. A particularly sensitive point was the future of the Romanovs. Before meeting the imperial family, Kerensky already had said, "I will not be the Marat of the Russian Revolution. I will take the tsar to Murmansk myself," referring to the Arctic port where he would put Nicholas and his family on board a British warship. In this expectation, the empress began sorting and packing and asked Dr. Botkin whether he would accompany them into exile in England. When King George V refused asylum to his Russian cousins, Kerensky looked elsewhere. It was to put them out of reach of the threatening Petrograd Soviet, not for poetic justice, that he sent the Romanovs to Siberia. He chose Tobolsk because it was a backwater without a railway, had a population which was prosperous, content, and old-fashioned, and possessed nothing remotely resembling an industrial proletariat. In addition, Tobolsk had a large provincial governor's residence suitable for housing the prisoners.

The family departed Tsarskoe Selo at dawn on 14 August 1917 in circumstances that were comfortable if not elegant. Their train consisted of wagon-lits of the International Sleeping Car Company, a restaurant car stocked with wines from the imperial cellar, and baggage compartments filled with favorite rugs, pictures, and knickknacks from the palace. In their portable jewel chests, the empress and her daughters carried diamonds, pearls, and other gems. In addition to the ladies and gentlemen of their retinue or suite, the Romanovs were accompanied to Siberia by two valets, six chamberlains, ten footmen, three cooks, a butler, a wine steward, two doctors, a nurse, two foreign tutors, a clerk, a barber, and a sailor from the imperial navy who for five years had carried and cared for the tsarevich. Three hundred and fifty veteran soldiers, picked from the Imperial Rifle Regiments and commanded by Colonel Eugene Kobylinsky, went along as an armed escort. Kerensky had given Kobylinsky a double mission: he was to guard the prisoners and prevent escape, but he was also to protect them from harm. On the night of their departure, Kerensky, who had come to Tsarskoe Selo to see them off, was asked by Count Paul Benckendorff, a minister of the court, how long they would stay in Siberia. He promised that, once the Constituent Assembly had met in November, Nicholas and his family would be free to go where they liked. By November, Kerensky himself had become a fugitive from Bolshevism.

The journey on the train, rattling eastward across the Urals, took four days. The mission and passengers were kept secret; the train, flying a Japanese flag and bearing placards proclaiming "Japanese Red Cross Mission," passed through towns and villages with blinds drawn and troops surrounding the station. At the end of each day, the train stopped in open country so that Nicholas and the children could descend for a walk; Alexandra remained in her compartment, fanning herself in the heat. In Tiumen, the passengers boarded a boat and began a two-day voyage up the Tura and Tobol rivers to Tobolsk.

At dusk on 19 August, the steamer docked at the wharf of the West Siberian Steamship and Trading Company and Kobylinsky went ashore to inspect the Governor's House, where the prisoners would live. He found it, Alexandra wrote in her diary, "empty and dirty and nothing arranged." The following morning, postponing the family's occupancy, Kobylinsky hired painters and paperers and bought furniture and a piano from families in Tobolsk. Electricians were summoned to improve the wiring, and plumbers came to install a bathtub. During the seven days it took to refurbish the house, the family lived aboard the boat. To break the monotony, the steamer made afternoon excursions along the river, stopping so that Nicholas and the children could walk along the bank. Finally, on 26 August, the house was ready, and at eight in the morning, the tsar, the tsarevich, and three of the grand duchesses walked from the dock to the house along a road lined with soldiers. Alexandra and Tatiana followed in a carriage.

Tobolsk, where the tsar and his family were to spend the next eight months, lay at the junction of the Tobol and Irtysh rivers. Once it had been a link with the Arctic and an important trading center for fish and furs. But the builders of the Trans-Siberian Railway had bypassed Tobolsk, going two hundred miles to the south, through Tiumen. In August 1917, when the imperial family arrived, the town was, as Kerensky had described it, "a backwater." Its twenty thousand people still made a living mostly from trade with the north. In summer, all transport was by river steamer; in winter, when the rivers were frozen, people traveled in sledges over the ice, or on paths cut through the snow along the riverbanks. The town itself was a sprawl of whitewashed churches, wooden buildings, and log houses scattered along streets that were thick with dust in the summer. In spring and fall, the dust turned to mud and the wooden planks laid down as sidewalks sometimes sank out of sight.

The Governor's House, a large, white, two-story building, fringed on every side with balconies, was the largest residence in town. Still, it was not large enough for the imperial party. The family moved into the mansion's main (or second) floor, with the four grand duchesses sharing a corner room and Nagorny, the tsarevich's sailor, sleeping in a room next to Alexis. The tsar and the tsaritsa shared a bedroom; in addition, she had a sitting room and he had a study. The tutor Pierre Gilliard lived on the ground floor downstairs in what had been the governor's study, and a number of servants were crammed into the attic. The remainder of the household lived across the street in a house owned by a merchant named Kornilov.

At first, Kobylinsky allowed the family considerable freedom of movement. On their first morning in the house, they all walked across the street to see how the rest of their party was settling into the Kornilov house. Some of the soldiers objected to this degree of freedom, and Kobylinsky reluctantly authorized the building of a high board fence which enclosed the house and a section of a small side street beside the house. The family subsequently took all its exercise within this muddy, treeless compound. Those who accompanied the Romanovs, on the other hand, were permitted to come and go freely, and several of the empress's maids took apartments in town. Dr. Botkin established a small medical practice in Tobolsk.

As Kerensky suspected, the people of Tobolsk remained strongly attached to the symbol and the person of the tsar. Walking past the Governor's House, they removed their hats and crossed themselves. When the empress appeared sitting in her window, they bowed to her. The soldiers repeatedly had to intervene and break up clusters of people who gathered in the muddy streets whenever the grand duchesses came out on a balcony. Merchants openly sent gifts of food, nuns from the local convent brought sugar and cakes, and peasant farmers arrived with butter and eggs. When the family was allowed to leave the house for the first time, to attend mass at the nearby Church of the Annunciation, a watching crowd stood behind a double cordon of soldiers. When the family passed—the tsar and his children on foot, the empress pushed in her wheelchair—many in the crowd made the sign of the cross and some fell on their knees.

By January 1918, Tobolsk was deep in a Siberian winter. At noon, the sun shone brightly, but by midafternoon the light had faded. The thermometer outside dropped to 68 degrees below zero Farenheit, freezing drafts blew through cracks in the doors and windows, and a glacial chill penetrated the walls. The girls' corner room became, in Gilliard's words, "a real ice house."[10] A fire burned all day in the drawing room, but the temperature inside the house never rose above 44 degrees. Sitting near the fire, the empress shivered, her fingers so stiff she could scarcely move her knitting needles. Outside, she saw "bright sunshine and everything glitters with hoar frost. . . . There are such moonlit nights it must be ideal in the hills. But my poor unfortunates can only pace up and down the narrow yard." Despite their circumstances, she said, the tsar was "simply marvelous. Such meekness while all the time suffering intensely for the country. . . . The others all good & brave & uncomplaining and Alexei is an angel . . . Anastasia, to her despair, is now very fat as Marie was, round and fat to the waist, with short legs. I do hope she will grow. Olga and Tatiana are both thin."[11]

Inside the Governor's House the imperial family settled into a routine which, although restricted, was almost cozy. The family ate a breakfast of tea and bread in the dining room downstairs at eight-thirty; Alexandra remained in bed and drank coffee. At nine, when Nicholas went to his study to read, the children's lessons began. Alexis was instructed in history and geography by Sidney Gibbs, an English tutor, and by the tsar. Alexandra gave German lessons three times a week to Tatiana and once a week to Marie. The empress also took on the teaching of religion to her children. Her program was extensive. Tatiana was assigned the books of Jeremiah, Ezekiel, Daniel, Hosea, and Joel. Marie read Joshua and Solomon, Anastasia read Isaiah, and Alexis, besides reading stories of David and Solomon, marched steadily through the gospels of Mark and Luke. (Olga, at twenty-two, was considered above schooling.) In addition to the Bible, Alexandra's students read a number of explanatory religious texts, including, in Alexis's case, Gogol's *Meditations on the Divine Liturgy.*

From eleven to noon, the tsar and children, usually accompanied by Gilliard, went out into the small courtyard for exercise. Nicholas, deprived of long walks, complained to Kobylinsky, who had tree trunks brought into the side yard. Thereafter, Nicholas and Gilliard, working with a two-man saw, cut wood for fireplaces and for heating water for baths. At one o'clock, the family assembled downstairs for lunch, although Alexandra usually ate in her room. After lunch, the tsarevich lay on a sofa while Gilliard read to him. At two, when the weather permitted, father and children went out again. While the tsar walked back and forth with his fast military step, his daughters hurried to keep up. At four-thirty, tea was served, after which the children's lessons resumed until six-thirty. Dinner at seven-thirty was followed by a gathering in the large hall for coffee or tea.

It soon became routine for the suite and the tutors to spend the evening with the family. Alexandra described the group in her diary as "we 7 [the imperial family], Nastinka [Countess Hendrikova], Trina [Schneider], Tatishchev, Valia [Dolgoruky], Mr. Gilliard, Mr. Gibbs, Dr. Botkin, [and] Dr. Derevenko." When the large hall became too cold, everyone took refuge in the imperial couple's drawing room, the warmest room in the house. Nicholas usually read aloud while Alexandra lay on a couch and did embroidery. Card games followed, often bezique, a version of pinochle. At nine, Alexis was sent to bed. At ten, his sisters followed, while the rest of the party remained together, sometimes until midnight.

It was Alexandra, sitting upstairs most of the day, who felt most acutely the passage of time and the change in their circumstances. She was aging rapidly (she was only forty-five), and her hair was gray. "I have grown quite thin. My gowns are like sacks," she wrote to Anna Vyrubova. "I read much and live in the past which is so full of memories. I sow [sew], embroider and knit with glasses because my eyes have become too weak to do without them." With her daughters, she made presents for Christmas: knitting woolen waistcoats for the suite and servants, painting ribbons for bookmarks, and making stockings for Alexis. "His are full of holes," she wrote. "I make everything now. Father's trousers are torn and darned; the girls' under linen in rags."

Alone in the house while the others were outside, Alexandra played the piano or sat on her balcony in the sunshine. "I can see all around me churches and hills, the lovely world. [There are] many churches around so we can always hear bells ringing." Sometimes, closing her eyes, she dreamed of English gardens. Mail still arrived with letters and packages from people far away: from Anna Vyrubova and others in Petrograd; from Nicholas's mother, dowager empress Marie, and his sisters Grand Duchesses Xenia and Olga in the Crimea. In January, as her children, one by one, succumbed to German measles, Alexandra again displayed her talent for nursing. And the prison regime still permitted her to receive medical help for herself: in the autumn of 1917, Dr. Kostrinsky, the former family dentist, arrived from the Crimea and devoted ten days to the empress's teeth. During the winter a local oculist came and supplied her with new eyeglasses.

Confinement bore most heavily on Alexandra in the form of denial of daily visits to church. Although a priest, a deacon, and nuns often came for evening prayer services in a corner of the downstairs drawing room arranged with icons and lamps, the absence of a consecrated altar made it impossible to hold mass. "We are not allowed to go to church on account of some kind of disturbance," Alexandra wrote Anna Vyrubova. "Nevertheless, church draws me irresistibly."

In spite of everything, Alexandra still considered herself Russia's empress. "When I sit in the window, the people bow to me if there are no guards present," she said. In these signs of respect, she found a continuing summons to duty. "I feel old, oh, so old, but I am still the mother of this country and I suffer its pains as my own child's pains and I love it in spite of all its sins and horrors . . . although Russia's black ingratitude to the emperor breaks my heart." And later, "The strange thing about the Russian character is that it can so suddenly change to evil, cruelty and unreason and can as suddenly change back again. . . . Russians are in reality big, ignorant children." The real reward, Alexandra believed, would come in another world. "One by one, all earthly things slip away, houses and possessions ruined, friends vanished. One lives from day to day. But God is in all, and nature never changes. . . . The more we suffer here, the fairer it will be on that other shore where so many dear ones await us."[12]

Not everyone in the Governor's House shared Alexandra's exalted fatalism. Her daughters—active, healthy young women between sixteen and twenty-two—were bored. "We often sit in the windows looking at the people passing," Anastasia wrote to Anna Vyrubova, "and this gives us distraction."[13] To enliven the long Siberian evenings, Gilliard and Gibbs proposed staging amateur Sunday evening theatricals made up of one-act plays in French, English, and Russian. A seven-week series began on 27 January with *Les Deux Timides,* a thirty-minute French play directed by Gilliard with a cast including the tsar, Prince Dolgoruky, Tatiana, and Anastasia. The audience consisted of the remainder of the family and suite, Dr. Botkin, Dr. Derevenko, Dr. Derevenko's son Kolia, and four maids. The following Sunday, Gilliard appeared, supported by Tatiana and Alexis, in a skit entitled *A La Porte.* Then came *La Bête Noire* with Tatishchev, Olga, Tatiana, Marie, and Countess Hendrikova. On 17 February, Gibbs took his turn, directing an English play entitled *Packing Up,* acted by Anastasia, Marie, and Alexis. Alexandra immensely enjoyed it. "Awfully amusing & really well and funnily given," she wrote in her diary; in fact, Gilliard reported, the empress had laughed so hard that she almost fell out of her chair. The weekly performances continued through 10 March with more plays in English and French and one in Russian, *The Bear* by Chekhov, in which Nicholas again appeared on stage. Thereafter, Lent brought these evenings of distraction to a close.

Meanwhile far away, the momentum of the revolution was accelerating. In November 1917, the Kerensky government had been overthrown by a Bolshevik coup d'état. At first, Nicholas, attempting to follow events in his newspapers, could not believe that Lenin and Trotsky posed any serious danger. They seemed to him to be a pair of blackguards, unsavory clowns, and—probably—traitors in the pay of Germany. When they suddenly vaulted to power, Nicholas was appalled. "For the first time, I heard the tsar regret his abdication," wrote Gilliard. "It now gave him pain to see that his renunciation had been in vain and that by his departure in the interests of his country he had in reality done her an ill turn. This idea was to haunt him more and more."[14]

Until January 1918, the changes in Petrograd and Moscow had little impact on distant Tobolsk. Commissar Vasily Pankratov, whom the tsarist regime had held in solitary confinement for fifteen years, was content to keep the prisoners restricted to the Governor's House; how they spent their days did not concern him. Colonel Kobylinsky, who commanded the soldiers, continued to balance keeping the prisoners from escaping and guarding them from harm. In mid-January, however, some of the soldiers became increasingly hostile and began to encroach on Kobylinsky's authority. An elected Soldier's Committee decided, by a narrow majority, that Nicholas could no longer be permitted to wear an officer's epaulettes. "At first it seemed as though the Czar would refuse" to comply, wrote Gilliard, "but, after exchanging a look and a few words with the Czarina, he recovered his self-control and yielded for the sake of his family."[15] Ten days later, on orders from Moscow, Commissar Pankratov was dismissed, and in mid-February most of the original veteran soldiers of the guard were demobilized and ordered to return home. The replacement soldiers dispatched to Tobolsk tended to be younger men who were more affected by revolutionary sentiments.

On 27 February, Kobylinsky received a telegram declaring that, as of 1 March, "Nicholas Romanov and his family must be put on soldiers' rations and that each member of the family will receive 600 rubles per month drawn from the interest of their personal estate." Nicholas asked Gilliard, Tatishchev, and Dolgoruky to do accounts and draw up a budget. The little committee looked for economies and recommended that ten servants be let go and that butter and coffee be excluded from the table. Alexandra also took an interest in the matter and, along with Tatiana and Marie, went over the accounts with Gilliard.

Through February, the newspapers were filled with reports of peace negotiations at Brest-Litovsk between Bolshevik Russia and Imperial Germany. Nicholas regarded this prospect with grief and shame; he called it "a disgrace" and "suicide for Russia." A year before, on leaving Army Headquarters after his abdication, he had said to the British military attaché, Maj. Gen. Sir John Hanbury-Williams, "Remember, nothing matters but beating Germany." Hearing a rumor that the treaty included a clause demanding that the tsar and the imperial family be handed over to Germany without harm, Nicholas called it "either a maneuver to discredit me or an insult." Defiantly, Alexandra added, "They [the Germans] must never dare to attempt any conversations with Father [Nicholas] or Mother [herself]. . . . After what they have done to the tsar, I would rather die in Russia than be saved by the Germans."[16] On 3 March, the Treaty of Brest-Litovsk was signed. Bolshevik Russia withdrew from the war, and the German army occupied all of Poland and one-third of European Russia.

That same month, sitting on her balcony in the early spring sunshine, sometimes wearing only a thin blouse and a silk jacket, Alexandra quietly began to hope. With the approach of Easter, she began to believe that some miraculous resurrection would come to Russia. "God will not leave it like this," she wrote to Anna Vyrubova. "He will send wisdom and save Russia, I am sure. . . . The nation is strong and young and soft as wax. Just now it is in bad hands and darkness and anarchy reign. But the King of Glory will come and will save, strengthen and give wisdom to the people who are now deceived."

This deliverance was not at hand. Instead, an old personal enemy rose up to smite Alexandra. Alexis had been relatively well during the autumn and winter; there were swellings in his knees and arms, but not much pain or incapacitation. For the tsarevich, the winter weather and family coziness had been exhilarating. "Today there are 29 degrees of frost, a strong wind and sunshine," he wrote to Anna Vyrubova. "We walked and I went on skis in the yard." Subsequently, he strained a ligament behind his left knee, but the tsaritsa reported no complications. At the end of January, he hurt his foot and this time suffered serious pain. As always, Alexandra remained with him day and night, having lunch and dinner by his bed. Alexis had a single playmate in Tobolsk, Kolia Derevenko, the son of his doctor, who had come to Siberia with his father, mother, and grandmother. In January, Kolia's visits became more frequent; often he arrived for tea and stayed for dinner. Within a week, Alexis was better. At the end of February, he hurt his toe, but that episode also passed quickly.

The worst blow occurred near the middle of April. On 12 April Alexandra wrote in her diary: "Baby stays in bed as fr. coughing so hard has a slight hemorrhage in the abdom." The hemorrhage worsened. The following day, the tsarevich suffered severely, vomiting repeatedly and sleeping only twenty minutes at a time. On 14 April, she recorded that he had "every half-hour very strong cramp-like pains." Alexandra remained with him throughout the day; Gilliard and others stayed with him at night. He began to improve; then, a week after the first attack, "far stronger pains today, only slept 20 m. in the day, no appetite, such suffering. Spent all day with him."

In a letter, Alexandra gave a more complete account to Vyrubova: "Sunbeam [Alexis] has been ill for the past week. I don't know whether coughing brought on the attack or whether he pushed up something heavy but he had an awful internal hemorrhage and suffered fearfully. He is better now but sleeps badly. The pains . . . have not entirely ceased. He is frightfully thin and yellow. . . . Yesterday he began to eat a little. The child has to lie on his back and he gets so tired. I sit all day beside him holding his aching legs and I have grown almost as thin as he. . . . Yesterday for the first time he talked with us and even played cards. He is frightfully thin with enormous eyes. . . . He likes to be read to, eats little. I am with him the whole day. Tatiana and M. Gilliard relieving me at intervals. M. Gilliard reads to him tirelessly."

On Monday 22 April, having first recorded that Alexis still was "terribly pale & thin," Alexandra noted in her diary that "more soldiers on foot & on horseback" were arriving almost daily in Tobolsk. It was impossible for her to know the importance of these arrivals, and that, as a result, she soon would be leaving her son behind for nearly a month. The reason was that Yakov Sverdlov, one of Lenin's senior lieutenants, had ordered Vasily Vasilevich Yakovlev to bring the tsar to Moscow. On 22 April, Yakovlev arrived in Tobolsk with 150 horsemen, as well as a private telegraph operator through whom he communicated directly with the Kremlin.

From the beginning an air of mystery attended this new commissar. On his first evening in Tobolsk, he had tea with the tsar and the tsaritsa but said nothing about his mission. He was around thirty-two years old, tall and muscular, with jet black hair. Alexandra wrote that he gave the "impression of an intelligent highly nervous workman [or] engineer." She and Nicholas further noted that, although Yakovlev was dressed as an ordinary sailor, he seemed to display a more cultivated background: his language was correct; he addressed Nicholas as "Your Majesty" and greeted Gilliard by saying "Bonjour, Monsieur." His hands were clean and his fingers long and slim.

Next morning, Yakovlev revealed his mission. He showed Kobylinsky his authorization and declared that any opposition by Kobylinsky or his soldiers meant instant death. Kobylinsky took Yakovlev to see Nicholas and Alexis. The tsarevich was lying in bed, his leg still badly drawn up from his recent hemorrhage. Later in the day, Yakovlev returned with an army doctor who assured Yakovlev that the boy was seriously ill and could not be moved.

On the morning of 25 March, Yakovlev discussed his dilemma with Kobylinsky. Originally, he had been assigned by the Central Executive Committee to bring the entire imperial family to Moscow. His discovery that the tsarevich was seriously ill had forced a reconsideration. He had communicated with Moscow. "Now, I have received an order to leave the family in Tobolsk and only to take the emperor away." He asked to see the tsar as soon as possible.[17]

"After lunch at two o'clock," said Kobylinsky, "Yakovlev

"We 7."—Alexandra's diary, 1 January 1918. The imperial family, c. 1915.

"Rested & wrote."—Alexandra's diary, 2 January 1918. Alexandra writing a letter in bed, Tsarskoe Selo, 1910 or 1911, photograph by Anna Vyrubova. Beinecke Rare Book and Manuscript Library, Yale University, Romanov Collection, album 7.

"In the morning I warmed myself while sitting on the greenhouse roof."—Nicholas's diary, 13 (26) January 1918. Nicholas with daughters on the roof of the greenhouse at the Governor's House, Tobolsk, early 1918. Beinecke Rare Book and Manuscript Library, Yale University, Romanov Collection, album 1.

"Drove through bystreets til reached a small house, around wh. high wooden pailings have been placed."—Alexandra's diary, 17 (30) April 1918. Exterior of the Ipatiev house, Yekaterinburg. fMS Russ 35, by permission of the Houghton Library, Harvard University.

"Always to be recognized by my sign 卍."—Alexandra to Anna Vyrubova, 16 December 1917. Inscription of reverse swastika and date found on the door jamb of Alexandra's room in the Ipatiev house. fMS Russ 35, by permission of the Houghton Library, Harvard University.

"Arrayed our Images on a table in the sitting room, for reading later."—Alexandra's diary, 19 April (2 May) 1918. Icons of the imperial family discovered in the Ipatiev house. fMS Russ 35, by permission of the Houghton Library, Harvard University.

"Luncheon, tea, supper as usual."—Alexandra's diary, 10 (23) May 1918. Dining room of the Ipatiev house. fMS Russ 35, by permission of the Houghton Library, Harvard University.

Semibasement interior of the Ipatiev house, site of the Romanovs' execution. fMS Russ 35, by permission of the Houghton Library, Harvard University.

and I entered the hall. The emperor and empress stood in the middle of the hall and Yakovlev stopped a little distance from them and bowed. Then he said, 'I must tell you that I am the Special Representative of the Moscow Central Executive Committee and my mission is to take all your family away from Tobolsk, but as your son is ill, I have received a second order which says that you alone must leave. The emperor replied, 'I refuse to go.' Hearing this, Yakovlev said, 'I beg you not to refuse. I am compelled to execute the order. In case of your refusal, I must take you by force or I must resign my position. In the latter case, the Committee would probably send a far less scrupulous man to replace me. Be calm. I am responsible with my life for your safety. If you do not want to go alone, you can take with you any people you wish. Be ready, we are leaving tomorrow [morning] at four o'clock.'"[18]

Yakovlev bowed again, first to the tsar, then to the empress, and left. As soon as he was gone, Nicholas summoned Kobylinsky and asked where he thought Yakovlev intended to take him. Kobylinsky did not know but said that Yakovlev had mentioned that the journey would take four or five days; therefore, he assumed the destination was Moscow. Nicholas nodded and, turning to Alexandra, said bitterly, "They want to force me to sign the Treaty of Brest-Litovsk. But I would rather cut off my right hand than sign such a treaty." The empress agreed and, grimly remembering the circumstances of the abdication, declared emotionally, "I shall also go. If I am not there, they will force him to do something in exactly the same way they did before."[19]

The news spread quickly through the house. Tatiana, in tears, knocked at Gilliard's door and asked him to come to her mother. The empress, greatly upset, told the tutor that the tsar was being taken the next morning and explained her own painful dilemma: "The commissar says that no harm will come to the tsar and that if anyone wishes to accompany him, there will be no objection. I cannot let the tsar go alone. They want to separate him from his family as they did before. They're going to try to force his hand by making him anxious about his family. The tsar is necessary to them; they feel that he alone represents Russia. Together, we shall be in a better position to resist them and I ought to be at his side in the time of trial. But the boy is still so ill. Suppose some complication sets in. Oh, God, what ghastly torture! For the first time in my life, I don't know what to do. I've always felt inspired whenever I had to make a decision and now I can't think. God won't allow the tsar's departure; it can't, it must not be."[20]

Tatiana, watching her mother, urged her to make a decision. "But, Mother," she said, "if Father has to go whatever we say, something must be decided."[21] Gilliard suggested that if she went with the tsar, he and the others would take excellent care of Alexis. He pointed out that the tsarevich was over the worst of the crisis.

"Her Majesty," he wrote, "was obviously tortured by indecision; she paced up and down the room and went on talking to herself rather than to us. At last she came up to me and said, 'Yes, that will be best. I'll go with the tsar. I shall trust Alexis to you.' A moment later the tsar came in. The Empress walked toward him saying, 'It's all settled. I'll go with you and Marie will come too.'"[22] In addition, Prince Dolgoruky, Dr. Botkin, the maid Anna Demidova, and the manservant Ivan Sednyov were to go with the imperial couple.

Meanwhile, Alexis was lying upstairs awaiting the visit his mother had promised to make after lunch. When she did not appear, he began to call, "Mama! Mama!" His shouts rang through the house even as Nicholas and Alexandra were talking to Yakovlev. When Alexandra still did not come, Alexis became frightened. Between four and five, she quietly came into his bedroom and explained to him that she and his father were leaving that night.

The entire family spent the rest of the afternoon and evening beside Alexis's bed. The empress prayed. At ten-thirty P.M. the suite came to join them for evening tea. They found Alexandra sitting on a sofa surrounded by her daughters, their faces swollen from crying. Nicholas and Alexandra were calm. At eleven-thirty they came downstairs to say good-bye to the servants. Nicholas embraced every man; Alexandra, every woman.

From the Kornilov house across the street, watchers saw the Governor's House ablaze with lights throughout the night. Near dawn, the clatter of horses and the creak of carriages signaled Yakovlev's arrival. The vehicles, which had to carry the party across two hundred miles of melting snow and mud to Tiumen, were crude baskets on wheels, more cart than carriage, lacking both springs and seats. Only one had a roof; in this, a mattress was placed for the empress to lie on.

When the family came downstairs, Alexandra, seeing Gilliard, begged him to go back up and stay with Alexis. The tutor went up to the boy's room and found him lying in bed, his face to the wall, weeping. After the cavalcade had left, Gilliard, sitting beside Alexis on the tsarevich's bed, heard Olga, Tatiana, and Anastasia climb slowly up the stairs and pass, sobbing, to their room.

Alexandra's diary description of the two-day, two-hundred-mile trip from Tobolsk to Tiumen needs little elaboration. Nicholas rode with Yakovlev, she and Marie together in another cart. She was "fearfully shaken, pain all over." At noon on the second day, they passed through the village from which Rasputin had come and, standing in the street while the horses were changed, they saw his family and friends looking at them from a window. Boarding a train in Tiumen on Palm Sunday, they departed, not westward toward Ekaterinburg, but to the east, toward Omsk, beyond which lay the Pacific, and safety. Yakovlev later explained that he had no intention of saving the tsar, but only took this route in order to bypass Ekaterinburg so that he could carry out his orders and deliver the prisoners safely to Moscow. If he traveled through Ekaterinburg, he feared the Ural Soviet might attempt to abduct his prisoners. Before reaching Omsk, however, the train was stopped and Yakovlev contacted Moscow. He was ordered to reverse direction, travel through Ekaterinburg, and, if the local soviet insisted, transfer the Romanovs to them.

The city of Ekaterinburg offered the Romanovs a grimmer reception and more ominous prospects than Tobolsk. The latter, still essentially a frontier town with an old-fashioned, conservative population, had greeted the former tsar and his family with curiosity, respect, and occasional reverence. Ekaterinburg, on the other hand, was already in 1918 a modern industrial city. Its population of 100,000 contained far greater extremes of wealth and poverty, and it displayed, accordingly, a much keener sense of economic grievance and political radicalism. Miners and factory workers, now triumphant and intent on righting wrongs, had brought the region the name of the Red Urals and given it a widespread reputation as one of the most independent and aggressively anti-monarchist territories of the new Bolshevik state. Nicholas was aware of these sentiments. When Yakovlev told him that their destination was Ekaterinburg, Nicholas said, "I would have gone anywhere but to the Urals. Judging from the local papers, people there are bitterly hostile to me."[23]

Near the center of Ekaterinburg, a successful merchant named N. N. Ipatiev had, around 1900, constructed a handsome, two-story house of white brick and heavy stone. The exterior of the house was designed in the style of old Muscovy with a carved façade and elaborate cornices. Behind these classical features, however, Ipatiev had greatly improved on the austere comforts of the old boyars (Muscovite noblemen) by equipping his house with modern plumbing and electric lights. Although Alexandra, on first arriving, described Ipatiev's house as "small," she saw it from the perspective of one accustomed to imperial palaces; in fact, the house possessed twenty-one rooms. The main rooms where Ipatiev and his family lived and received were on the second floor. Below, built into a hill, the lower story was made up of some rooms at street level and other rooms, almost cellars, half-buried in the earth.

Near the end of April 1918, the Ural Soviet abruptly ordered Ipatiev to leave his house. As he was departing, workmen began erecting a board fence fourteen feet high, enclosing the house and the small garden behind. Nicholas, Alexandra, and Marie entered Ipatiev's house on 30 April. Alexandra's diary describes the six-hour wait in the railway yard while Yakovlev negotiated the delivery of his prisoners to the Ural Soviet, Prince Dolgoruky's separation from the family (he was imprisoned and, later that summer, shot), the trip in an open motorcar followed by a truckload of heavily armed soldiers through back streets of the city, a late lunch of soldier's rations in the form of a bowl of borscht brought from a local hotel, and, eventually, after Nicholas had read aloud from the Bible, the end of their first day in the house.

They arrived at the Ipatiev house on Tuesday of Passion Week, and, despite their circumstances, the prisoners immediately began preparing for Easter, the holiest day in the Orthodox calendar. Nicholas read aloud from the book of Job, his patron saint. On Holy Thursday, he and Dr. Botkin took turns reading aloud the story of Christ's Passion from the four gospels. On Saturday night, a priest and deacon were permitted to come to perform the traditional Orthodox midnight service, ending in the proclamation by the priest, "Christ is risen!" and the response of the worshippers, "He is risen, indeed!"

Biblical stories of suffering and Calvary had a growing significance inside the Ipatiev house. Upon arriving, Alexandra noticed that the guards were new. In fact, the Ipatiev house now had two distinct sets of guards. On the street outside the fence, the guard consisted of ordinary Red soldiers. Inside the house, the guards were special Bolshevik zealots picked from revolutionary Ekaterinburg factory workers. The leader of this inner guard, Alexander Avdeev, was a tall, thin-faced man who habitually referred to the former tsar as "Nicholas the Blood Drinker." A few months before, Avdeev had personally arrested the owner of the factory in which he worked. He hated the tsar and told his men that Nicholas had forced Russia into war solely in order to spill the blood of a greater number of workers. Avdeev drank heavily, went beltless and unbuttoned, and encouraged his followers to do likewise. On the excuse of examining the family's baggage, Avdeev and his men thoroughly pilfered the family's baggage stored in a downstairs room.

At first, the weather exhilarated Alexandra. In May, Siberia was turning to spring and the empress was joyful that the long winter seemed over. "Glorious, so warm & sunny," she wrote on 30 April, the day they entered the Ipatiev house. Thereafter: "Beautiful, warm, sunny, but windy . . . glorious bright sunshine . . . sunshine and clouds change about . . . beautiful warm morning . . . sat in the garden . . . warm wind. . . ." Spring was fickle, however, and on 25 May she reported that it was "snowing hard" and the next day that "everything [was] covered by snow."

After the beginning of their third week, it became difficult for the prisoners to see the snow on the ground from inside the house. On 15 May, Alexandra reported, an old man had painted over their windows from the outside with white paint so that they could only see the sky; the effect from inside was that they were in a thick fog. The following day, another man painted over the outside thermometer so that they were unable to read the temperature. Four days later, the commander of the guard scratched off the paint so that they could again see how warm or cold it was.

For the first eight days in Ekaterinburg, Alexandra had no word from her children in Tobolsk. She wrote to them daily, sometimes twice a day; in fact, thirty-four times in twenty-three days. On 8 May, a telegram from Tobolsk told her that all was well. One of the empress's letters advised "disposal of the medicines as had been agreed." By prearranged code, "medicines" meant jewels. The fortune in gems brought from Tsarskoe Selo had been left behind in Tobolsk because Nicholas and Alexandra, given only a few hours' notice by Yakovlev, had not had time to hide them on their own persons. Receiving this message, the three daughters in Tobolsk began sewing diamonds, emeralds, amethysts, and pearls into the lining of their underclothing and hats. Removing the buttons from their woolen dresses, they made new buttons by taking jewels, wrapping them in black silk, and sewing them onto the clothes.

On 19 May, Olga, Tatiana, Anastasia, and Alexis departed Tobolsk. The river ice had melted and the *Rus,* the same steamer which had carried the Romanovs up the river the summer before, brought the children and the remainder of the suite and servants back downstream to Tiumen, where they were put aboard a train for Ekaterinburg. Once again, when the train arrived at the station in Ekaterinburg, there was a selection process: the four children, Nagorny, the cook Kharitonov, a manservant Trupp, and a kitchen boy Leonid Sednyov (a nephew of the servant who had arrived earlier with the tsar) were sent to the Ipatiev house; General Tatishchev, Countess

Hendrikova, Trina Schneider, all Russians, were arrested (and later shot); the two foreign tutors, Gilliard and Gibbs, were allowed to go wherever they wished. In the Ipatiev house, the children's arrival brought a burst of happiness and a shuffle of rearrangements. There were not enough beds, and that night Marie slept with her sisters on cloaks and cushions on the floor so that Alexis could have her bed. Kharitonov slept on a sofa, and little Leonid Sednyov slept across two chairs.

Thereafter, the tsar, his family, and members of their household were confined to five upstairs rooms. Nicholas and Alexandra had the corner bedroom, furnished with pale yellow wallpaper, two beds, a couch, two tables, a lamp, a bookcase, and a single armoire which held their clothing. Their four daughters and thirteen-year-old son shared another room (eventually, Alexis's bed was moved into his parents' room). The maid, Anna Demidova, slept in the dining room, Dr. Botkin slept in the salon, and Trupp and Kharitonov were in a large hallway. Two or three armed guards were always present on the main floor with the family, and in order to go to the washroom and toilet, the captives had to walk past these men.

The prisoners settled into a monotonous routine. Every morning the family rose at eight and assembled for morning prayers. Breakfast was black bread and tea. The main meal arrived around two P.M. when soup and cutlets, sent from a local soviet kitchen, were rewarmed and served by Kharitonov. Tea was served at five, supper at eight. Usually, Nicholas read aloud to the family after tea and in the evening; as the electricity was often turned off at night, the family read and played cards by candlelight. Those who wished were permitted to walk in the garden, forty steps in either direction, twice a day: thirty minutes in the morning, thirty minutes in the afternoon.

The family's joy at being reunited was quickly overshadowed by the illness of the tsarevich. The day the children arrived from Tobolsk, Alexandra wrote in her diary: "Baby woke up every hour from pain in his knee, slipped & hurt it when getting into bed. Cannot walk yet, one carries him. [He has] lost 14 pounds since his illness. . . . Tore sinews in the knee most probably."

From that day to the end, Alexis's illness dominated his

mother's thoughts. Mother and son had most of their meals in her bedroom. The tsarevich's physician, Dr. Derevenko, who again had been permitted to go about freely, was allowed to make occasional visits to his patient. During the seventy-eight days they spent in the Ipatiev house, Derevenko was the only outside person close to the family who was authorized to enter. To make certain that no messages passed by this channel between the prisoners and the outside, the doctor was allowed to come and examine his patient only in the presence of Avdeev. When Avdeev was unable to be present, Derevenko was not permitted to come, no matter how ill the boy was.

At first, the tsarevich slept in a room with the sailor Nagorny, who sat up with him when the boy was in pain. Dr. Botkin then appealed to Avdeev to ask the Ural Soviet that Gilliard be allowed to come to the Ipatiev house to help care for the tsarevich. In response, Avdeev brought four men to look at Alexis. When they left, the appeal was rejected. That night, Botkin sat up part of the night with the boy so that the exhausted Nagorny could sleep.

On 27 May, four days after his arrival in the Ipatiev house, Nagorny was taken away, along with the elder Sednyov. As the tsarevich's caretaker stepped out of the house surrounded by Red Guards, Gilliard, Gibbs, and Dr. Derevenko happened to be walking past in the street. "Nagorny was going to the carriage," wrote Gilliard. "He was just setting foot on the step . . . when raising his head, he saw us all there standing motionless a few yards from him. For a few seconds he looked fixedly at us, then without a single gesture that might have betrayed us he took his seat. The carriages were driven off . . . in the direction of the prison."[24] The next day, Alexandra asked Avdeev when they could have Nagorny back. Avdeev replied that he did not know. Alexandra confided to her diary that she feared they would never see either Nagorny or Sednyov again. Her foreboding was well placed: four days later, Nagorny and Sednyov were shot. The family was never told.

Eventually, as the bleeding in Alexis's knee stopped and the fluids were reabsorbed, his pain subsided and his leg began to straighten. When the weather was good, Botkin, Trupp, Kharitonov, or Marie carried him outdoors to sit in the sun.

"Wheeled Baby into the garden & we all sat there for an hour," Alexandra wrote on 18 June. "Very hot, nice lilac bushes & small honeysuckle, quite pretty foliage, but as untidy as ever."

Most of the time, Alexandra, like Alexis, remained indoors, immobilized. Her head ached, her eyes ached, she felt dizzy. On 31 May, she "remained [the] whole day with shut eyes, head got worse towards the evening." Unable to walk, she lay in bed or sat in her wheelchair in the pale yellow bedroom and stared at the white-painted windows. When she could, she embroidered, drew, read her Bible, her prayer books, and religious texts. Her daughters took turns caring for her: Marie read to her and washed her hair; Tatiana and Anastasia read to her; Olga stayed indoors with her when the others went out to walk. Alexandra herself found new things to do. On 28 May, she recorded, "I cut Nicholas's hair for the first time"; and on 20 June she cut it again. She worried about Prince Dolgoruky, of whom they had had no news. Surprisingly, some mail and a few newspapers continued to arrive. To Alexandra's delight, her sister Grand Duchess Elizabeth (Ella) sent coffee and chocolate, and the following morning, the empress reported she had had a "great treat, a cup of coffee." Simultaneously, she learned that Ella had been sent from Moscow to Perm in the Urals. (The night after the annihilation of the imperial family, this other Hessian princess was murdered along with four other Romanovs.)

Unable to go out when he wished, Nicholas paced his room. One warm evening in June, he wrote in his diary, "It was unbearable to sit that way, locked up, and not be in a position to go out into the garden when you wanted and spend a fine evening outside." Suffering from hemorrhoids, he went to bed for three days in June "since it is more convenient to apply compresses." After two days and nights, he sat up and the next morning, got up and went outside. "The green is very fine and lush," he wrote in his diary.

Birthdays were noted, but scarcely celebrated: on 19 May, Nicholas was fifty; on 6 June, Alexandra was forty-six; on 18 June, Anastasia turned seventeen; on 27 June, Marie, nineteen. (On 4 June, Alexandra reported that the new ruler of Russia had exercised his power even over the clock and, to save electricity, put the nation on daylight saving time.) With the passage of time, isolation and physical proximity created a new social entity, and the captives, from tsar and empress to doctor and cook, merged into an extended family. Botkin, now an old friend, sat with Nicholas and his wife after supper to talk and play cards. During the day, when Alexandra and Alexis could not leave the house, Botkin remained inside with them for card games. After Nagorny was removed, Botkin sometimes slept in the room with the tsarevich, and he shared with Nicholas, Trupp, Kharitonov, and even Marie the task of carrying the boy down the stairs and into the garden. On 23 June, Botkin himself became violently ill with colic, requiring an injection of morphine. He remained sick for five days; when he was able to sit up in an armchair, Alexandra sat with him.

June brought summer heat. Sudden thunderstorms with lightning and sheets of rain were followed quickly by bright sunshine and greater heat. On 6 June, Alexandra noted, "Very hot, awfully stuffy in rooms." The kitchen made things worse: "Very hot, stuffy as no windows open and smells strong of kitchen everywhere," she reported on 17 June. Four days later, she wrote: "Out in the garden, fearfully hot, sat under the bushes. They have given us . . . half an hour more for being out. Heat, airlessness in the rooms intense."

Closed windows made the heat stifling. In order to keep the prisoners from escaping or signaling to the outside, all of the white-painted double windows in the family rooms were kept shut by order of the Ural Soviet. The tsar set himself to overturn this decree. "Today at tea, six men walked in, probably from the Regional Soviet, to see which windows to open," he wrote in his diary on 22 June. "The resolution of this issue has gone on for nearly two weeks! Often various men have come and silently in our presence examined the windows." On this issue, Nicholas II triumphed. "Two of the soldiers came and took out one window in our room," Alexandra wrote on 23 June. "Such joy, delicious air at last and one window no longer whitewashed." The prisoners crowded to the open window to inhale fresh air. "The air in the room became clean, and by evening, cool." "The fragrance from all the town's gardens is amazing," her husband said.[25]

Beyond the Ipatiev house—beyond Ekaterinburg—Russia was convulsed by civil war. In numerous regions, the Bolsheviks, who had moved the capital from Petrograd to Moscow, confronted various military groups of anti-Bolsheviks, none of whom were specifically monarchist. In Siberia, in the early summer of 1918, the anti-Bolshevik Whites were in the ascendant and had seized several cities and towns not far from Ekaterinburg. In Ekaterinburg, the Ural Soviet, aware of its own deteriorating position, worried about what to do with the Romanovs. On 13 June, Avdeev suddenly told the family that, because of a threat by "anarchists," they must pack their belongings and be ready to leave. They spent the afternoon and evening packing, only to be told at midnight that the anarchists had been captured and they would not be leaving. Avdeev, who was drunk, also promised that Nagorny and Sednyov, both dead, would be returned to them within three days.

In the sunlight, Alexis sat quietly while Nicholas and his daughters walked under the eyes of the guards. In time, the guards' impressions of the family began to change. "I have still an impression of them that will always remain in my soul," said Anatoly Yakimov, a member of the guard later captured by the Whites.

> The tsar was no longer young, his beard was getting grey. . . . [He wore] a soldier's shirt with an officer's belt fastened by a buckle around his waist. . . . The buckle was yellow . . . the shirt was khaki color, the same color as his trousers and his old worn-out boots. His eyes were kind and . . . I got the impression that he was a kind, simple, frank and talkative person. Sometimes, I felt he was going to speak to me. He looked as if he would like to talk to us.
>
> The Tsaritsa was not a bit like him. She was severe looking and she had the appearance and manners of a haughty, grave woman. Sometimes we used to discuss them amongst ourselves and we decided that she was different and looked exactly like a tsaritsa. She seemed older than the tsar. Grey hair was plainly visible on her temples and her face was not the face of a young woman. . . .
>
> All my evil thoughts about the tsar disappeared after I had stayed a certain time amongst the guards. After I had seen them several times, I began to feel entirely different towards them; I began to pity them. I pitied them as human beings. I am telling

> you the entire truth. You may or may not believe me, but I kept saying to myself, "Let them escape . . . do something to let them escape."[26]

On 4 July, a "lovely morning, nice air, not too hot," the president of the Ural Soviet, Aleksandr Beloborodov, appeared and abruptly dismissed Avdeev and his factory-worker guards. A new commandant, whom Nicholas called "the dark gentleman," took control of the Ipatiev house. This man, who had black eyes, black hair, and a black beard and who wore a black leather jacket, was the Chekist Yakov Yurovsky. At first, Yurovsky's arrival heralded minor improvements in the prisoners' situation. The new Cheka guards were better disciplined, and petty harassment of the grand duchesses on their way to the toilet ceased. Yurovsky collected and made lists of the jewelry and gold ornaments worn by the family, returned some of the objects pilfered by Avdeev's men, sealed everything in packets, and left them for the family to keep. Within a few days, however, when Yurovsky's men began to cover the only open window with a heavy iron railing, Alexandra described him as "harsh," and Nicholas said of him, "We like this man less and less."

Ironically, on the day Yurovsky arrived, Alexandra recorded that Alexis was getting better: "Baby eats well & is getting heavy for the others to carry cruel they wont give us Nagorny back again. He moves his leg easier." On 13 July, Alexandra noted that, "At 6:30, Baby had his first bath since Tobolsk. He managed to get in & out alone, climbs also in & out of bed, but can only stand on one foot as yet." This was a glimmer of hope, but the pervading atmosphere was one of growing despair. The change was noted by an Ekaterinburg priest who had been permitted once before to enter the Ipatiev house to perform a service. Father Storozhev had come on 23 June, and Yurovsky had agreed that he could come again. On his first visit, he had noted that although Alexandra seemed tired and ill, Nicholas and his daughters were in good spirits. Alexis, unable to walk, had been carried to the service on a cot. He seemed happy when Father Storozhev approached with the crucifix, the boy looked up at him with bright, curious eyes.

On Sunday, 14 July, when the priest returned, the change was marked. The priest found the family waiting together, all of them anxious and depressed. Alexis was sitting in his mother's wheelchair. Alexandra, wearing a lilac dress, sat beside him. Nicholas, in khaki field shirt, trousers, and boots, was standing with his daughters, who were dressed in white blouses and dark skirts. When the deacon sang the prayer "At Rest With the Saints," the family kneeled and one of the girls began to weep. This time when the crucifix was brought to Alexis, the priest found him pale and thin, lying in a white nightshirt with a blanket covering him up to the waist. His eyes, looking up, were clear, but sad and distracted.

By the middle of July, a White Russian army, bolstered by thousands of anti-Bolshevik Czechs, was approaching Ekaterinburg. The prisoners knew that something was impending; on the twelfth Alexandra reported hearing infantry, cavalry, and artillery passing in front of the house; on the thirteenth she heard three revolver shots; on the fifteenth, artillery and more revolver shots.

Tuesday, July 16, the family's last day, began as a gray morning which brightened into sunshine. The family gathered, prayed together, and had tea. Yurovsky arrived to make his inspection and, as special treat, brought fresh eggs and milk for Alexis, who had a cold. When Yurovsky took the kitchen boy, Leonid Sednyov, away from the house, Alexandra wondered whether they would ever see him again. In mid-morning, Nicholas, Olga, Marie, and Anastasia went out for half an hour while Tatiana stayed behind to read to her mother from the prophets Amos and Obadiah. At four in the afternoon, Nicholas and his four daughters walked again in the garden. At eight, the family had supper, prayed, and then separated; Olga, Tatiana, Marie, and Anastasia went to their room; Alexis went to bed in his parents' room. Alexandra stayed up to play bezique with Nicholas. At ten-thirty, she recorded the day's events in her diary. Her last entry was the temperature. It was cool, she wrote: "15 degrees" (58 degrees F.). Then, for the last time, she closed her diary, lay down, and went to sleep.

NOTES

1. Lili Dehn, *The Real Tsaritsa* (London: Thornton Butterworth, 1922), 39–40.
2. Pierre Gilliard, *Thirteen Years at the Russian Court* (New York: Doran, 1921), 72.
3. Gilliard, *Thirteen Years,* 26.
4. Ian Vorres, *The Last Grand Duchess: The Memoirs of Grand Duchess Olga Alexandrovna* (London: Hutchinson, 1964), 130.
5. Colonel Eugene Kobylinsky, deposition, quoted in Robert Wilton, *The Last Days of the Romanovs* (London: Thornton Buttonworth, 1920), 219.
6. Anna Vyrubova, *Memories of the Russian Court* (New York: Macmillan, 1923), 105.
7. Vyrubova, *Memories,* 109–110.
8. Dehn, *The Real Tsaritsa,* 165.
9. Alexander Kerensky and Paul Bulygin, *The Murder of the Romanovs* (London: Hutchinson, 1935), 122–123.
10. Gilliard, *Thirteen Years,* 253.
11. Vyrubova, *Memories,* 314–316.
12. Vyrubova, *Memories,* 313.
13. Vyrubova, *Memories,* 309.
14. Gilliard, *Thirteen Years,* 243.
15. Gilliard, *Thirteen Years,* 252.
16. Gilliard, *Thirteen Years,* 257.
17. Kobylinsky quoted in Wilton, *Last Days,* 205.
18. Kobylinsky quoted in Wilton, *Last Days,* 205.
19. Kobylinsky quoted in Wilton, *Last Days,* 206.
20. Gilliard, *Thirteen Years,* 260.
21. Gilliard, *Thirteen Years,* 261.
22. Gilliard, *Thirteen Years,* 261.
23. P. M. Bylcov, *The Last Days of Tsardom* (London: Martin Lawrence, 1934), 72.
24. Gilliard, *Thirteen Years,* 272.
25. Nicholas's diary, quoted in Edvard Radzinsky, *The Last Tsar: The Life and Death of Nicholas II* (New York: Doubleday, 1992), 317.
26. Quoted in Wilton, *Last Days,* 274–275.

The 1918 Diary of Tsaritsa Alexandra

Jonathan Brent

THE 1918 DIARY OF TSARITSA ALEXANDRA FYODOROVNA is more properly called a daybook, following the suggestion of the English word *AGENDA* imprinted on the cover of her earliest extant diary, from 1887. As such, the *Tagebuch für Alix von Hessen,* as she later styled it, was never intended to be a record of her emotional experiences or her deepest reflections. Going back to the 1880s, when she began to keep a diary as a teenager, the future tsaritsa noted where she was, whom she had seen, and what she had done. Only rarely did she comment on the quality of her experience and then only in the most cursory fashion. After Nicholas's fall from power, she often noted, simply, "Everything as usual," or "Lunched as usual." She made a point of observing the weather at exact times throughout the day.

As it was for many young women of noble or even middle-class birth in the late nineteenth century, keeping her diary became early on for Alexandra a daily habit of pinpointing herself in time and space along a number line that extended from yesterday to today to tomorrow, thus producing a true log of her individual reality and existence. The uninscribed pages of her 1918 diary which follow the family's execution on the night of 16–17 July 1918, with the dates she had clearly written in at the top, offer their own mute pathos and ironic witness to Alexandra's fate, that of her family, and that of the imperial world she represented.

Her earliest entries are written in English with an admixture of German, which appears less and less frequently after her marriage. She is always scrupulous in noting her place of residence, the time of day at which she writes her entry, and the correlation of numerical date with day of the week. In the first entry for 1891, 1 January is a Thursday. She is in Darmstadt. She writes her diary entry at 8:07 P.M. She goes with Papa at 8:00 A.M. to the Stadtkirche. She notes the family members with whom she celebrates the new year. The only personal perception she offers is that the actors in the performance of Shakespeare's *Tempest* that she attended "acted well." Then came supper and "To bed."

Her days followed one another methodically with a regularity integral to the calm procession of imperial time. It was not the time of shopkeepers, laborers, or those busied by the hurly-burly of this world. Her world had the almost clocklike precision of a courtly dance. What to us may seem its boring, merely empty repetitiveness was the sign of its tranquil, unhurried continuity: the ritual of her daily life. Page after page of the 1918 diary shows her lunching at twelve or one, having tea at four-thirty, resting at six, usually dining with the children at eight, and at nine playing bezique with Nicholas, who often read to the family. "Dined with Baby," "Nicholas read to us," and "Rested & wrote" are phrases that recur in these pages like a litany, the basso continuo of a life whose tragic drama is being played out in higher registers.

At the time of her engagement to Nicholas in 1894, Alexandra expressed an idiosyncratic interest in numbers and coded language which continued throughout her life and may help to explain certain important features of her 1918 diary. On 16 April 1894 she writes: "At 5 went to the station, to receive (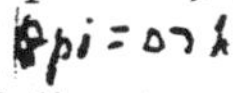) Ella, Serge, Nicholas, Heidi. . . ." Her entry for the following day begins: "After breakfast went to Ella. Sat with Nicky.  . . . ." Entries of the same sort appear throughout the year.

Attempting an explanation of this code is beyond the scope

of this brief essay. It is sufficient to observe that the future empress constructs a private language of numbers, Greek letters, and quasi-algebraic equations. Indirectly this violates the notion that her diary recorded nothing more important than the weather or the minor events of the day. Alexandra's recourse to this private language makes of these thoughts and feelings something "top secret," the sanctum sanctorum of an emotional experience she could not put into words for herself. Although her letters to trusted friends demonstrate that she was capable of freely and fully articulating her perceptions, her diary suggests a complicated relationship to herself.

Twenty-four years later, in 1918, the same sensibility makes itself felt, though in a modified form. The dates, temperatures, and hours, set down like a numbered code with Germanic exactitude, do not now tell the story of a powerful romantic encounter but rather recount a life-and-death struggle with the transforming power of the Revolution. Whatever Alexandra's reasons for adopting this style of composition, by virtue of it her 1918 diary becomes a secret text. Through the irony of history, this text—whose secrets Alexandra hoped to keep from her Bolshevik captors—was held by them also to be a top-secret text (*Sovershenno sekretno*) in the Soviet archives for some seventy-five years after her death. Secrets perpetuate secrets.

It had been Alexandra's habit to bring both the moment she awoke and the moment she lay down to sleep into relation with the outside temperature and the temperatures of her sick children. Thus the 1918 diary begins with her notation that it was −4 degrees (Celsius) on Monday, 1 January, the Feast of the Circumcision. She arises at seven-fifteen. At eight she goes to church. Olga's temperature is 37.3 degrees. Does Alexandra wake up early or late? Is Olga feeling better or not? Is −4 degrees unseasonably warm or cold? These questions do not concern her here.

Rather, Alexandra's numbers express and organize her world. The empress had long made a practice of assigning a number to each item of correspondence she composed to friends and loved ones. Thus on 2 January she writes in her diary, "Mme. Syroboiarskaia No. 17. Lili [Den]: No. 4." On 4 (17) May, after a prolonged separation from her children,

Coburg.

Monday.
16. April

At 5 went to the station, to receive
(8⁰⁰=07h.) Ella, Serge, Miechen, Vladimir, Paul & Nicky. Went to
Schloss where they all live.
Dined a. Marie at 7½, & then
to Theatre "Vogelhändler". – Spoke
to Ernsy sbinny. — Kitty,
Steinbock, Schilling, Kotzenbey. –

106

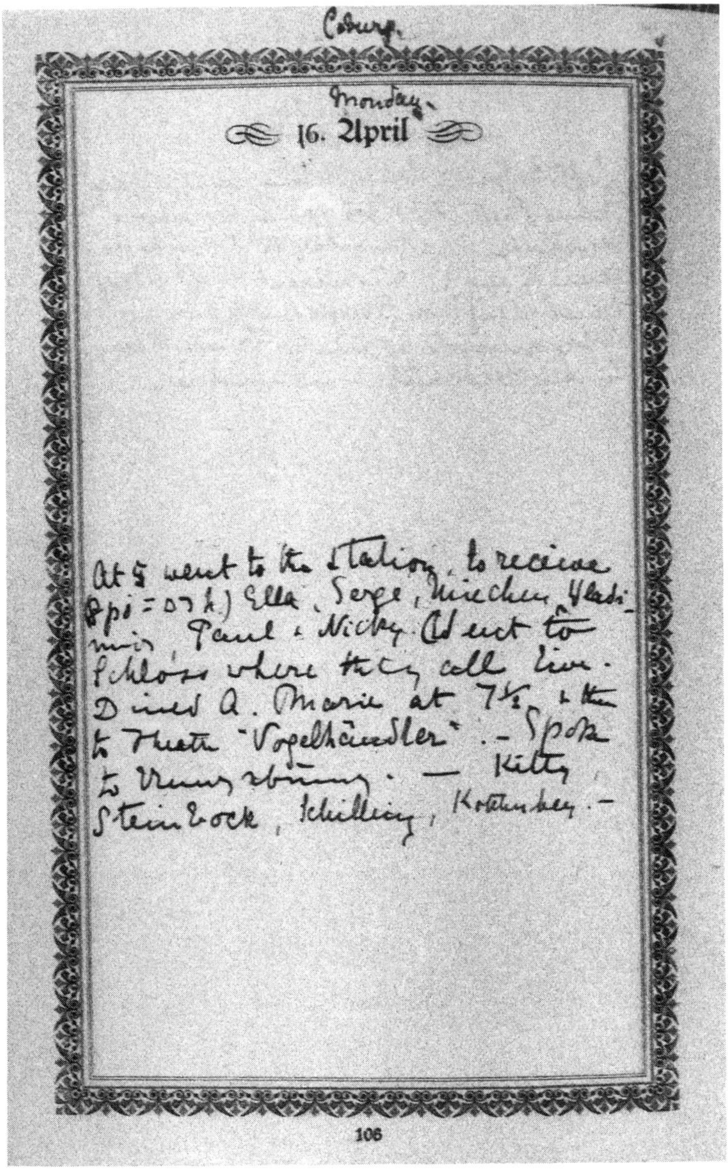

Alexandra's diary entry for 16 April 1894.

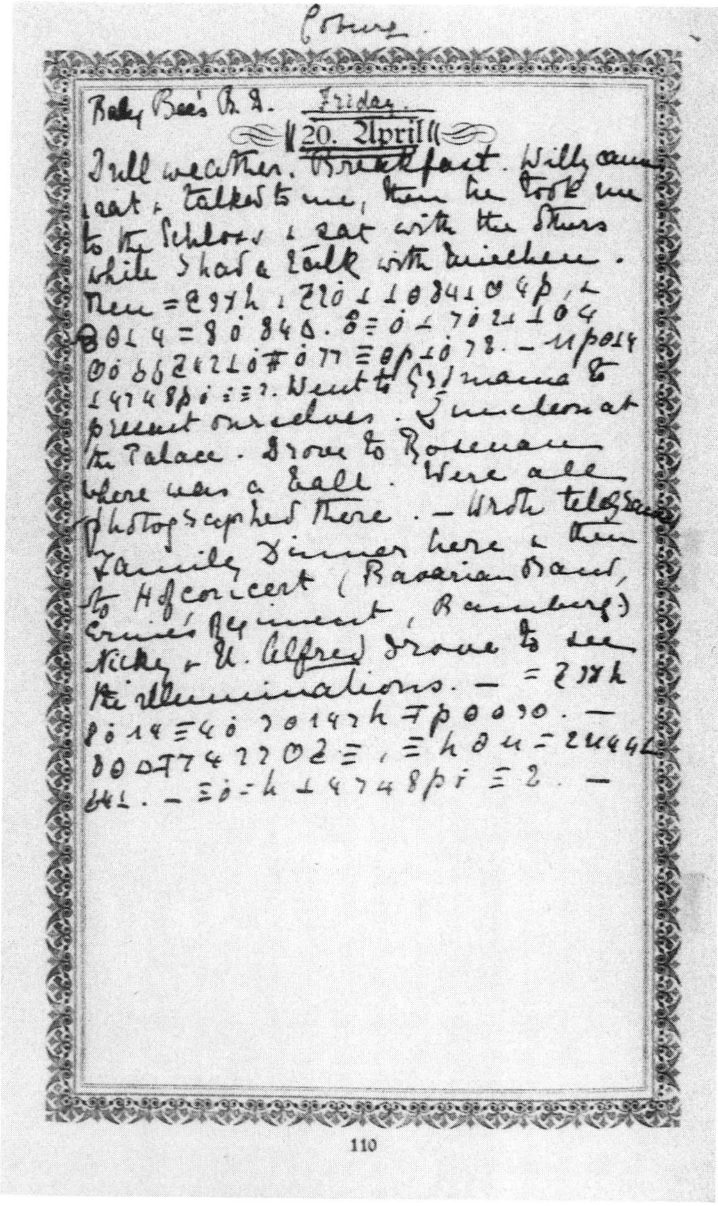

Coburg.

Baby Bee's B.D. Friday.

20. April

Dull weather. Breakfast. Willy came & sat & talked to me, then he took me to the Schloss & sat with the others while I had a talk with [illegible]. Then [illegible] Went to [illegible] mama to present ourselves. Luncheon at the Palace. Drove to Rosenau where was a ball. Were all photographed there. — Wrote telegrams. Family dinner here & then to Hofconcert (Bavarian Band, Ernie's Regiment, Bamberg.) Nicky & U. Alfred drove to see the illuminations. — [illegible]

110

Alexandra's diary entry for 20 April 1894.

she writes: "Maria Wrote 22 time to the children." She likewise often observes not simply the names but the *number* of her company, as for instance in her 1 January entry, "We 7." In the same spirit, she notes that 2 January marks the "3rd anniversary of Ania's accident."

As a frontispiece to the diary, Alexandra wrote out the Cyrillic Old Church Slavonic alphabet. Under each letter she placed its numerical value. She closes the majority of her first one hundred entries with a letter from this sacred alphabet along with its corresponding number, as if to encode her own passage through the mundane cycle of days and hours with a larger mythic and religious journey. She finally abandons this device after the one-hundredth day, 10 (23) April. This was two days before the family is separated and she is forced to accompany Nicholas to Yekaterinburg—the point at which she might well have begun to perceive that some vital connection to the past was irrevocably severed.

Although the Old Church Slavonic alphabet evokes a reverenced tradition, the empress's sense of the present is signaled by an additional number owing to the transition from the Julian to the Gregorian calendar. The new calendar was inaugurated officially by the Bolshevik government on 1 February 1918, yet it had been unofficially in use for some time. The third of January marks Alexandra's first use of the Gregorian calendar in her diaries. But this new dating system is conjoined to the old, which she does not relinquish—-a fact of no little symbolic and psychological importance. Each day henceforth bears a double date in the form of a fraction: 3 January, old style, becomes the numerator, and 16 January, new style, becomes the denominator. Alexandra's representation of this double date, as well as her representation of positive and negative indoor and outdoor temperatures by writing numbers above and below a line, graphically suggests her deeper engagement with the question of lines of division, lines of demarcation, thresholds of experience.

As the German-born granddaughter of Queen Victoria, at home in both English and German languages, and then an ardent convert to Russian Orthodoxy, the empress was no stranger to crossing the arbitrary lines of a divided world. But now she depicts daily experience not only in German and English (or English and Russian) but simultaneously and insistently as something defined by two different dates, often two different months, two different hours, both inside and outside temperatures. Her world is one in which she is constantly approaching a threshold—the line or limit graphically represented in her notation of time, temperature, day, and year. This threshold is one she encountered in all her daily tasks, from taking tea to celebrating church holidays. Depicted day after day in the 1918 dairy, this recurrent imposition of the line, the sense of arbitrary division in all her activities, produces the overwhelming impression of a woman living in two worlds—the old and the new, the ancient and the modern, the domestic and the imperial, the sacred and the profane, the quotidian and the apocalyptic—whose most mundane distinctions she scrupulously manages. By contrast, Nicholas is much more inconsistent in his use of the double dating system in his diaries. He adopts it on 1 (14) February but abandons it on 18 (31) March when he reverts again to the old style. Alexandra, it seems, was grounded in both worlds, whereas Nicholas was much more bound to only one.

The day the empress inscribes the new order in her diary, 3 (16) January, is followed exactly six months later on 3 (16) July by her execution, when she crossed another line of demarcation. This was mere chance, of course, but it becomes suggestive when seen in the context of Alexandra's passion for numerological progressions and anniversaries—as if precisely six months were necessary for the moment of her intellectual acceptance of the new calendar to be actualized in her corporeal death.

It was not the mere fact of enforced idleness in Tobolsk and Yekaterinburg that gave such regularity and order to Alexandra's diary. She did not live an eventless or routine life during these last seven months, yet the character of her diaries remains substantially the same from before the Revolution to the time of her confinement in Yekaterinburg. The diary, therefore, cannot be read as simply a "record" of events. Nor is it the product of mere lifelong habit. Rather, through her customary effort of observation and memory Alexandra continually constructed and reconstructed the past *form* of her life in the face of her present circumstances. It is not personal identity she affirms so much as a transpersonal, symbolic order of well-being and permanence. Did Alexandra simply not wish to recognize the collapse of her world? Or did she encode that perception in this final diary in the same way that she had encoded her 1894 meetings with Nicholas?

The form of her diary is stubbornly maintained throughout this tumultuous period, but it is not merely mechanical. Elements of the diary change over time, but its character does not. She introduces and then discontinues certain habits or routines. Others she revives. After her first entry on 1 January, she does not note the hour she awakens until 14 (27) April, when she journeys to Yekaterinburg, and not again until 23 May (5 June), when she observes that she "got up at 6:30, now 8:30" because of the recent Bolshevik decree instituting daylight saving time. Although virtually every entry contains the time she takes tea, has lunch, goes to sleep, or attends a church service, her concern for Aleksei's suffering or her own physical exhaustion leads to inconsistency. She uses Old Church Slavonic letters and numbers, which she had not previously employed and after a certain point does not return to. We see her introduce the Gregorian calendar even while continuing scrupulously to observe each church holiday.

Alexandra's diary brings the inexorable, predetermined succession of days, anniversaries, hours, and minutes—numbers following one another seemingly without end—into relation with the daily, unpredictable contingencies of the weather, her children's temperatures, and the chaotic events of the Revolution. We see the empress presiding over a world within a world, which is given simple form in her daily observations. In this transparent, almost invisible structure we see her thinking; we come to know the shifts of her mind and the conscious concessions by which she attempts to preserve the spirit of the ancient order in the profane and atheistic new world that declared obsolete the very orthography of that order. As the tsar and his family watched their retainers grow ever fewer, as they burned their letters and saw iron bars secured over their windows, as the daughters sewed their jewels into their corsets, and as the family prepared themselves for a denouement they could neither foresee nor forestall, the 1918 diary remains Alexandra's link to her past, even as it projects a future she could not inhabit. It was a past, however we may wish to judge it, whose character was determined by precisely that sense of order, decorum, and ritual which is the essence of her daily observations.

Therefore, although Alexandra's incessant jottings of time, place, weather, holidays, and anniversaries may seem, at first glance, of little or no importance, they are, upon reflection, what give this little book unique significance as a text. The diary records not only the empress's own day-by-day descent into the maelstrom of revolution and the modern world, but principally her symbolic accommodation of the new and her resistance to the destruction of a traditional order of thought, action, and belief. Her death was a representative death which proved synonymous with the death of the old calendar itself.

Imperial time is swallowed up in revolutionary time, just as the old calendar is displaced by the new. It is possible to trace this in the empress's diary at moments when the exigencies of the imperial world collide painfully with those of the Revolution which has engulfed it. At these points, the staid regularity of the diary gives way to a far less orderly recounting of the course of events. Perceptions, fears, and anxieties press in upon Alexandra on 12 (25) April, when she commits to her diary Commissar Yakovlev's ultimatum that Nicholas must transfer from Tobolsk to some unknown destination: "(if not willing then obliged to use force)," she writes. "I had to decide to stay with ill Baby or accompany him. Settled to accompany him as can be of more need & too risky not knowing where & for what. (we imagine Moscow) Horrible suffering. Marie comes with us, Olga will look after Baby, Tatiana the household & Anastasia will cheer all up."

Gone here is the precision of her earlier notations about the weather, her time for taking breakfast or lunch, and when she retires for the night. Though these remain preoccupations, the *form* of the diary now muddles them together with impressions of the world that are breaking fast in upon her. The next day of travel, Friday 13 (26) April—not an insignificant combination for someone numerologically inclined—is recounted in an extended entry in which the ultimate fate of Alexandra and her family seems to make itself indirectly felt. "One does not tell us where we are going," she complains.

The travel and separation of the family, however temporary, summon up, in Alexandra's hurried account, a sense of the larger transition through which Russia itself is now passing: "Road perfectly atrocious, frozen ground wind, snow, water up to the horses' stomachs, fearfully shaken, pain all over." At this point, the daybook form of the diary collapses, just as the carriages in which the empress rides lose their wheels, the family loses its cohesion, and Russia itself disintegrates into civil war verging on chaos: "By turn each carriage lost a wheel or something else smashed. Luggage always late.—heart aches, enlarged, wrote to the children through our first coachman."

Olga, Tatiana, Anastasia, and Aleksei do not rejoin their parents until 10 (23) May, after a painful month long separation—Alexandra notes that it was exactly "4 weeks" since they had left Tobolsk. During this first month that she, Nicholas, and Maria spent in Yekaterinburg, the diary resumes its previous regularity. But in the days following the other children's appearance, the diary again loses its shape. The form of Alexandra's entry for 10 (23) May, as much as its content, tells of the confusing intensity of their reunion caused by the illness of the tsarevich and the Bolsheviks' ominous new encroachments on the family's imperial prerogatives. Aleksei "cannot walk yet, one carries him. Lost 14 pounds since his illness." But then the empress observes: "Saw fr. far in the night great fire burning." On 13 (26) May, she notes: "Lunch was brought again late." The house was searched by the Bolshevik guards. The tsarevich's "swelling is a little less. No news of our people." On 22 May (4 June), Alexandra writes with irritation: "Lenin gave the order that the clocks have to [be] put 2 hours ahead (economy of electricity) so at 10 they told us it was 12." For Alexandra, time is now completely out of joint.

Hereafter, Alexandra struggles to reimpose the old form of the diary, something that became increasingly difficult as the Romanovs lose more and more control over events. While the imperial family's own personal possessions were being relentlessly inventoried by their Bolshevik captors, down to the bracelets Alexandra could not remove, Alexandra's own efforts to take the measure of all things in her world—the time, the weather, her children's temperatures, the number of gunshots heard in the night—reinvent a powerful symbolic connection to the imperium in which she and Nicholas were believed to be the last intercessors of God on earth. To those sharing the empress's faith, their deaths signified the loss of not merely two absolute monarchs but the world's concrete link to the Divine.

Fate and numbers are often associated. Friday the 13th is unlucky; 7 is lucky. But there is also the Old Testament book of Numbers, whose first chapters are devoted to the counting of the Israelites, and the apocalyptic number 666 of the Antichrist, of which Alexandra would have been keenly aware. We can only speculate on what fascination or compulsion lay behind the numbers so abundant in her private diary. What we do know is that she counted her days and numbered them, even as her days were numbered by forces she could not control or comprehend. The Bolsheviks conceived the Revolution as the consummation of history; Alexandra entered a different apocalyptic time—the "great fire" burning in the night—while observing the days, hours, and minutes as they passed. She recorded the temperature of her children and of the weather. The last notation of her hand was "15 degrees." Neither Kafka nor Beckett could have memorialized with greater irony the death of the old imperial order or the birth of the new time and space wrought by the Revolution.

Editorial Note

The editors have tried to preserve the character of Alexandra's diary while making certain concessions to readability. The diary is for the most part in English, but she freely alternated between the Roman alphabet and the Cyrillic (Russian) alphabet, using Russian to write most proper and geographical names and many isolated words (including ecclesiastical terms and medical terms relating to Aleksei's treatment). Alexandra's literate Russian summaries of Aleksei's Old Testament lessons, as a rule, are the only complete Russian sentences in the diary. The Russian has been translated in almost all cases.

The idiosyncrasies of Alexandra's spelling, grammar, punctuation, and capitalization; her use of Arabic numerals for numbers and Old Church Slavonic Cyrillic to number her diary pages; and her heart, cross, and swastika symbols have all been retained. Abbreviations of common words have been retained where they are unlikely to cause misunderstanding (*fr.* for from, *m.* for minutes, *p.c.* for post card, etc.). However, abbreviated proper names have been completed without the use of brackets (*N.* is Nicholas, *Al.* is Aleksei, *Turg.* is Turgenev, etc.). Alexandra "encoded" the names of the correspondents to whom she wrote on a given day at the bottom of that day's diary entry. She often used only a single letter followed by the sequential number of the letter she sent (*A. 5* signifies her fifth letter to Anna Vyrubova, for example). Where the editors could identify the correspondents with sufficient certainty, complete names have been substituted for the initials in the entry. Where some doubt remains or a name has eluded identification, it is reproduced as in the original.

Alexandra double-dated the headings of her diary entries in both old and new styles as of 3 January 1918. Her device for noting the old date (Julian calendar) in the numerator and the new date (Gregorian calendar—adding thirteen days) in the denominator has been reproduced in this volume. Where dates in the notes, glossary, and chronology are double-dated, old style appears first, followed by new style in parentheses. Otherwise, the dates are generally those in use at the time: old style for dates before February 1918, new style for dates following 1 (14) February 1918 (the official adoption of the Gregorian calendar).

Alexandra's use of fractions to indicate partial hours (e.g., 4¾) has been standardized (4:45).

All temperatures noted by Alexandra are in degrees Celsius. Her use of an overbar or underbar to indicate air temperatures below or above zero, respectively, has been rendered by the familiar symbols (e.g., −25°).

With the exception of the Introduction, Russian names of people, places, and institutions have been transliterated according to a modified Library of Congress system—without soft signs and with a simplified handling of vowels. For some people with well-known names in English (for example, Nicholas and Alexandra), the common English name is used. Because the regular Library of Congress system is familiar to researchers, it is used for source citations and for Russian terms and phrases.

In the notes, all sources and documents cited have been translated from the Russian, with the exception of Pierre Gilliard's diary, which is quoted (with certain corrections) from F. Appleby Holt's translation from the French (New York, 1921). In rendering Russian Orthodox liturgical terms in English, the editors have consulted the *Liturgical Calendar and Rubrics for the Year 1997* (St. Tikhon's Seminary Press).

Timothy D. Sergay

THE LAST DIARY OF TSARITSA ALEXANDRA

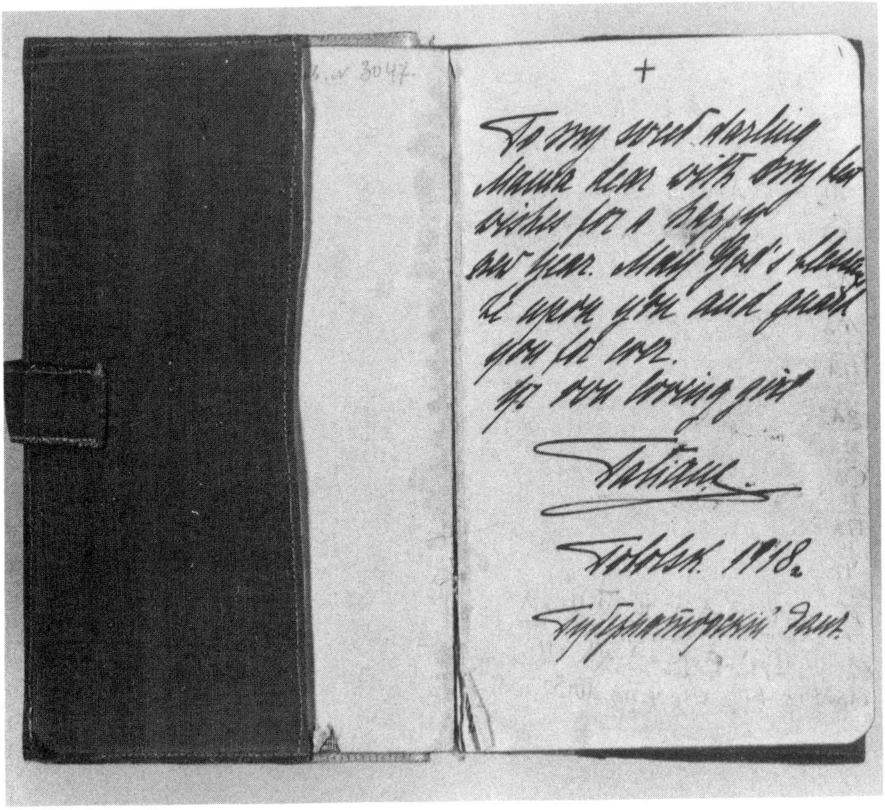
3047
Tobolsk. 1918.

†

To my sweet darling Mama dear with my best wishes for a happy new year. May God's blessings be upon you & guard you for ever.

yr own loving girl

Tatiana.

Tobolsk. 1918

Governor's House.

1918.

҂а ц и҃і.

а҃.	в҃.	г҃.	д҃.	є҃.	ѕ҃.	з҃.	и҃.	ѳ҃.	і҃.
1.	2.	3.	4.	5.	6.	7.	8.	9.	10.
а҃і.	в҃і.	г҃і.	д҃і.	є҃і.	ѕ҃і.	з҃і.	и҃і.	ѳ҃і.	к҃.
11.	12.	13.	14.	15.	16.	17.	18.	19.	20.
к҃а.	к҃в.	к҃г.	к҃д.	к҃є.	к҃ѕ.	к҃з.	к҃и.	к҃ѳ.	л҃.
21.	22.	23.	24.	25.	26.	27.	28.	29.	30.
л҃а.									
31.									
м҃а.									
41.									
н҃а.									
51.									
ѯ҃а.									
61.									
ѻ҃а.									
71.									
п҃а.									
81.									
ч҃а.									
91.									
р҃.	с҃.	т҃.	ѵ҃.	ф҃.	х҃.	ѱ҃.	ѿ҃.	ц҃.	҂а҃.
100.	200.	300.	400.	500.	600.	700.	800	900.	1000.
҂а	҂в	҂т	҂д	҂є	҂к	҂л	҂м	҂н	
1000.	2000.	3000.	4000.	5000.	20,000.	30,000.	40,000.	50,000.	
с҃лє.	т҃нз.	ф҃пѕ.	х҃чє.	ѱ҃мд.	ѿ҃ог.	ц҃кв.			
235.	357.	586.	695.	749.	873.	922.			

TOBOLSK I JANUARY †

Circumcision of the Lord

−4° MONDAY

7:15. Got up. At 8 went to Church.

Olga in bed 37.3°. Tatiana too 38°. German measles (rubella) Tatiana has a strong rash all over, headache & eyes bloodshot. Aleksei alright again Sat with the girls, sowing. I lunched with them in their bedroom at 12. Beautiful, sunny weather, sat on the balcony for 35 m: & then with the girls til tea-time

4:30. Kolia Derevenko also took tea.

6:00. rested til 8, reading & writing.

2:00. Olga 37.4° Tatiana 38.5°

6:00. " 37.5° " 38.7°

8:00. Dined with Olga & Tatiana.

9:00. Olga 37.7° Tatiana 38.5°

Played bezique with Nicholas, then he read to us & I knitted.—

We 7, Nastinka, Trina, Tatishchev, Valia Dolgorukov, Mr. Gilliard, Mr. Gibbs, Dr. Botkin, Dr. Derevenko (& Isa) are here.— Mother dear, Olga husband & Tikhon, Xenia & family are all at Ai Todor.

Numbers from 10–20: first the units, then the tens
Numbers from 20–100: first the tens, and then the units
Numbers from 100–1,000: first the hundreds, then the tens and units.

1. А҃.

Church: The Church of the Annunciation in Tobolsk. The Liturgy was celebrated by Fr. Vladimir Khlynov, replacing Fr. Aleksei Vasiliev, who had been censured by the Tobolsk Soviet for authorizing the traditional wish for long life to the imperial family during services on 25 December 1917. *37.3°:* On the Celsius scale, a normal temperature is 37°, the equivalent of 98.6° Fahrenheit. *rubella:* The children most likely caught rubella from Aleksei's twelve-year-old playmate Kolia Derevenko. *We 7:* Nicholas, Alexandra, and their five children. Since 1891 Alexandra noted family members' whereabouts in the first diary entry of the new year (Mushits, 4). *Mother dear:* The dowager empress Maria Fyodorovna, Nicholas's mother. *Olga husband & Tikhon:* Grand Duchess Olga Aleksandrovna, Nicholas's younger sister; her second husband, Nikolai Kulikovsky; and their infant son, Tikhon. *Xenia:* Grand Duchess Ksenia Aleksandrovna, the elder of Nicholas's two sisters. *Ai Todor:* The Crimean estate of Grand Duke Aleksandr Mikhailovich. *Numbers:* Instructions for writing numerals in Old Church Slavonic Cyrillic, referring to the table on the facing page in her diary.

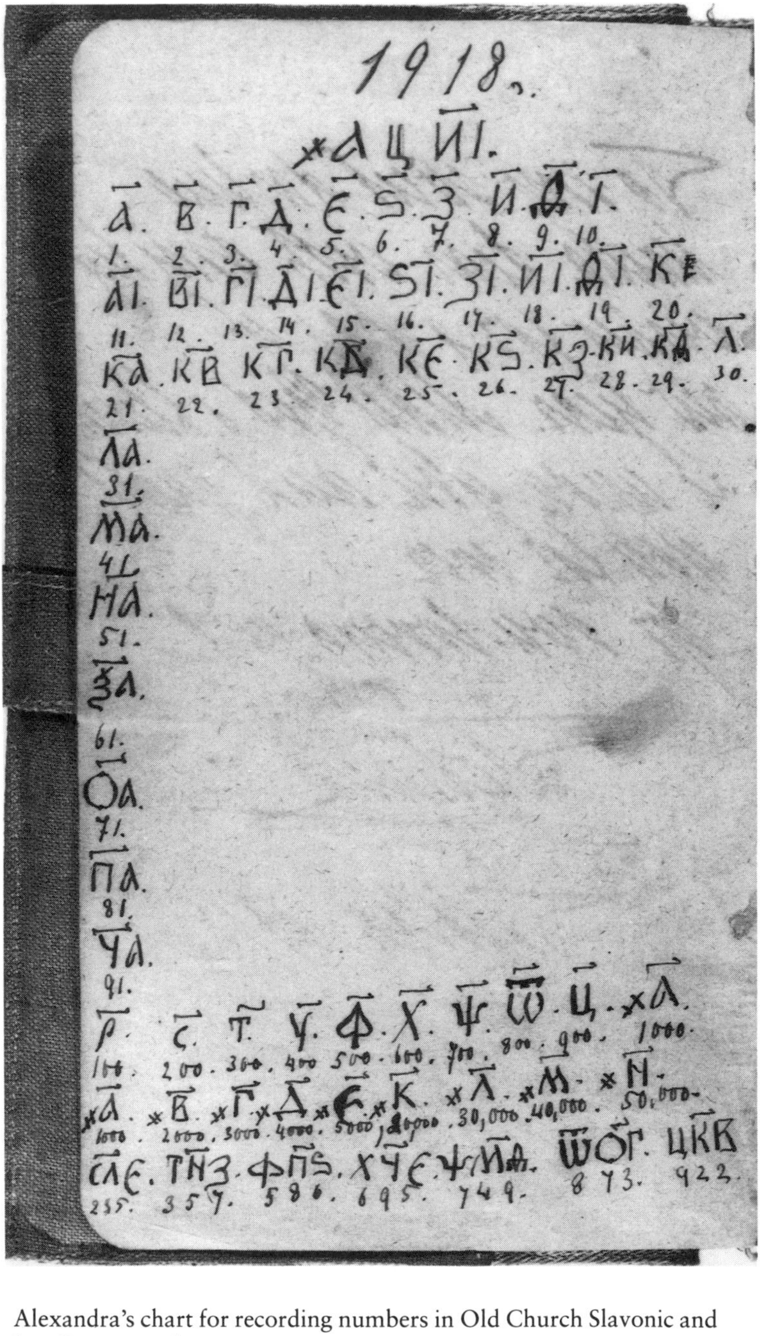

Alexandra's chart for recording numbers in Old Church Slavonic and her diary entry for 1 (14) January 1918.

Тобольскъ.

4 — **1. Январь.** Обрѣзаніе Господне. Понедѣльникъ. 2

7 1/4 got up. At 8 went to church.
Ольга in bed 37.3. Татьяна too 38. German measles (краснуха) Татьяна has a strong rash all over, headache & eyes bloodshot.
Алексѣй alright again.
Sat with the girls, sewing.
Lunched with them in their bedroom at 12.
Beautiful, sunny weather, sat on the balcony for 35 min. & then with the girls til tea time
4 1/2 Костя Деревенко also took tea.
6. Алексѣй til 8, reading & writing.
2. Olga 37.4. Tatiana 38.5.
6. " 37.5. " 38.7.
8 ч. Dined with Olga & Tatiana.
9 ч. Olga 37.7. Tatiana 38.5.
Played bezique with N., then he read to us & I knitted. —

At 7 Настинка, Трина, Татищевъ, Баронъ Б., Mr Gilliard, Mr Gibbs & Dr Botkin, Dr Деревенко (& Isa) are here. —
Motherdear, Olga husband & Тихонъ, Xenia & family are all at Аи Тодоре.

Числа отъ 10–20 составл. сперва ставятся един.: а пот. десятки
числа отъ 20–100 сперва пишутъ десятки, потомъ един.
числа отъ 100–1000, сперва сотни, потомъ десятки а единицы.

TOBOLSK 2 JANUARY

St. Serafim

−5° TUESDAY

Olga: 37.5° Tatiana 37.1° Olga's rash now strong. Tatiana coughs & sneezes. Sat with the children.

1:00. lunched with Olga & Tatiana.

2:00. Olga: 38.4° Tatiana: 36.9°

Sat with Olga & Tatiana.

4:30. tea.

6:00. Olga 38.3½° Tatiana 36.9°

Rested & wrote.

3rd anniversary of Ania's accident.

8:00. Dined with Olga & Tatiana

9:00. Olga 38.4½°—Tatiana 36.8°

Nicholas finished reading *Nest of the Gentry.*—

Mme. Syroboiarskaia: No. 17. Lili: No. 4.

2. Б.

St. Serafim: The Orthodox Church commemorated the Repose of St. Serafim, Wonderworker of Sarov. Alexandra attributed the birth of Aleksei to Serafim's intercession with God. *Ania's accident:* On 2 January 1915, Alexandra's lady-in-waiting Anna (Ania) Vyrubova had suffered injuries in a train accident (see glossary). *Nest of the Gentry:* Novel (1859) by Ivan Turgenev. Nicholas customarily read aloud to the family in the evening after supper.

TOBOLSK 3/16 JANUARY

−5° WEDNESDAY

Olga: 37.4° Tatiana. 36.4° Aleksei 36.2° has also got rubella.

Sat with the children.

1:00. Lunched with Olga, Tatiana & Baby.

Snowed slightly, went out for half an hour.

Sat with the children, & Klavdia Mikhailovna comes every day. worked.

4:45. tea. bezique with Anastasia—

6:00. Olga: 37.2° Tatiana: 36.6° Aleksei: 36.1°

Rested.—Officers & soldiers have been obliged to take off their epaulettes & stripes.

The soldiers absolutely forbid Isa & Madelaine, Annushka & Niuta to come to our house. The latter three are here waiting since 4 week & Isa since over a week.

8:00. Dined in the girls bedroom with Olga, Tatiana & Aleksei—Tatiana half up all day.

9:00. Olga 37.7°

Nicholas read to us Turgenev

Syroboiarsky No. 8

3. Г̄.

3(16) January: Henceforth Alexandra records calendar dates in her diary in both old and new style, while Nicholas as a rule used the old style only. *comes every day:* Klavdia Mikhailovna Bitner tutored the children (see glossary). *epaulettes:* Nicholas's diary: "The committee of the rifle detachment decreed the removal of epaulettes in order not to be subjected to insults and attacks in town. Incomprehensible! *The soldiers absolutely forbid:* Commissar Pankratov (see glossary) refused to admit Baroness Buksgevden (Isa) and three personal maids who had arrived from Petrograd on 5 December to the Governor's House on the grounds that there were already enough domestics. *Madelaine:* Magdalina Frantsevna Zanotti, the empress's senior personal maid, went voluntarily into exile in Tobolsk.

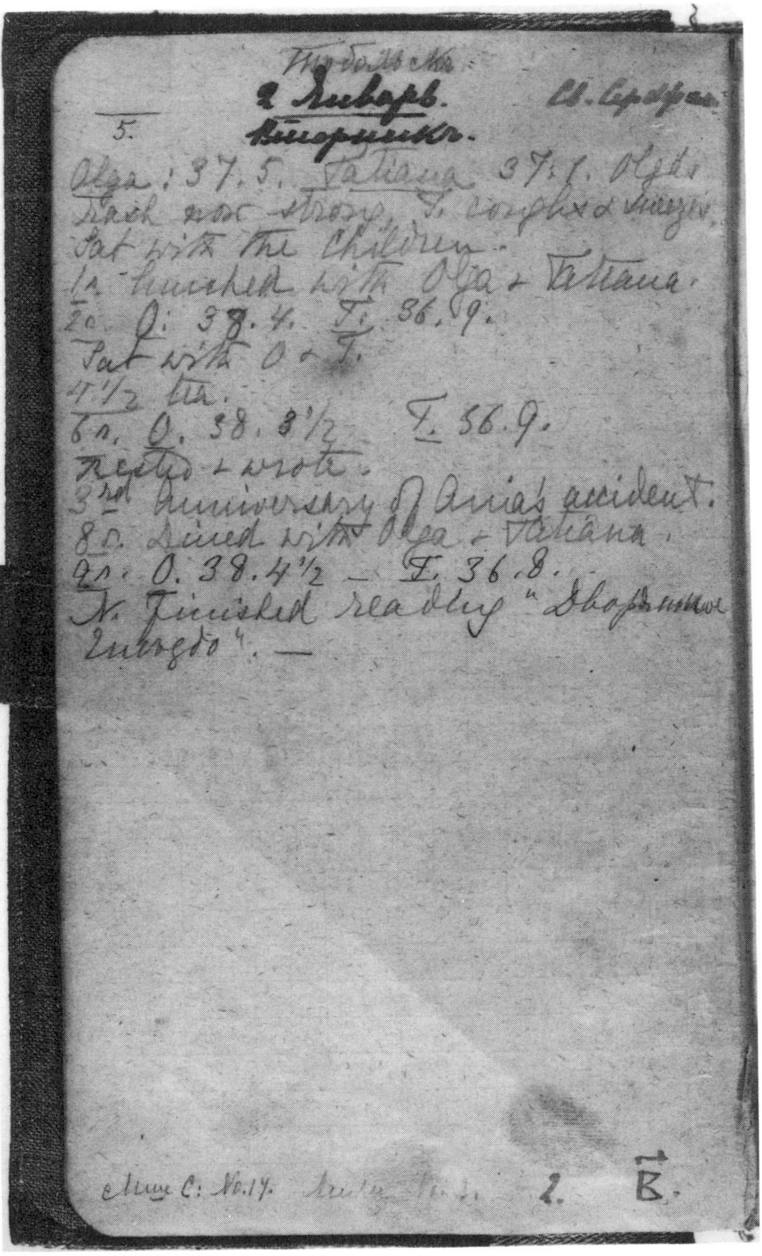
Тобольскъ.
2 Январь. Св. Серафима
5.
Вторникъ.
Olga: 37.5. Tatiana 37.1. Olga's back not strong, T. coughs & sneezes.
Sat with the Children.
1 p. lunched with Olga & Tatiana.
2 p. O: 38.4. T: 36.9.
Sat with O & T.
4 1/2 tea.
6 p. O. 38.3 1/2 T. 36.9.
Rested & wrote.
3rd anniversary of Ania's accident.
8 p. dined with Olga & Tatiana.
9 p. O. 38.4 1/2 — T. 36.8.
N. finished reading "Дворянское гнездо". —

Alexandra's diary entries for 2 (15) and 3 (16) January 1918.

Тобольскъ

5 3го Декабрь
Среда

Olga: 37.4. Татьяна. 36.4. Алексѣй 36.2. has also got краснуха.
Sat with the Children.
1 ч. Lunched with Olga, Tatiana & Baby,
Snowed slightly, went out for half an hour.
Sat with the children, & Klavdichin: comes every day. worked.
4 3/4. tea. - bezique with Anastasia
6 ч. O: 37.2. Т: 36.6. Al: 36.1.
Yesterday. - Officers & soldiers have been obliged to take off their погоны & шашки.
The soldiers absolutely forbid Isa & Madelaine, Аннушка & Кюнна to come to our house. The latter three are here waiting since 4 week & Isa since over a week.
8 ч. Dined in the girls bedroom with O, T & Al. - T. half up all day.
9 ч. O. 37.7.
N. read to us Тургенев

TOBOLSK 4/17 JANUARY

−8° THURSDAY

Marie has got the German measles too:

Olga: 36.8° Tatiana: 36.1° Maria: 38.2°
Aleksei: 36.4°

Sat with the Children—

Lunched with Olga, Tatiana, Maria & Aleksei.
−10°

2:00. Olga: 36.7° Maria 39

Sat with the girls—& with Baby.

6:00. Olga: 36.6° Maria 39.5° Aleksei 36.3°

Klavdia Mikhailovna sat with the girls.

Rested. Kolia came as usual.

8:00. Dined with Olga, Tatiana, Maria & Aleksei.

9:00. Olga 36.5½°—Maria: 38.8°

Nicholas read to us, I worked as usual.

Mme. Syroboiarskaia No. 18. p.c. thr. Niuta

4. Д̄.

I worked: Apart from the children's formal studies, Alexandra and her daughters pursued painting, embroidery, knitting warm articles of clothing for gifts, photography, and reading. *p.c. thr. Niuta:* To evade censorship and not attract the attention of the guards, Alexandra sometimes conducted her correspondence with the aid of retainers who were living in town.

TOBOLSK 5/18 JANUARY

−7° FRIDAY

Olga: 36.6° Maria: 36.9°:

2:30. Lunched with Olga & Marie.

Tatiana & Aleksei lunched downstairs.

I went out for half an hour into the kitchen garden, talked to the soldiers (4th regiment.)

3:15. Blessing of the Waters and vespers—

new Priest—blessed the rooms.

4:30. tea. Kolia too. Olga up.

Rested. 2:00. Maria: 36.4°

6:00. Maria: 36.6°

8:00. dined with Olga & Marie.

9:00. Maria 36.7½°

Nicholas read to us.

5. Є̄.

new Priest: Fr. Khlynov (see note for 1 January). This date is the Eve of the Theophany (Western Epiphany). Pierre Gilliard's diary: "The priest and choir arrived at 3 o'clock. To-day is the Blessing of the Waters and the first time the new priest has officiated in the house. When it was Alexis Nicolaievitch's turn to kiss the cross held out by the priest the latter bent down and kissed his forehead. After dinner General Tatichtchef and Prince Dolgorouky came to beg the Czar to remove his epaulettes in order to avoid a hostile demonstration by the soldiers. At first it seemed as though the Czar would refuse, but, after exchanging a look and a few words with the Czarina, he recovered his self-control and yielded for the sake of his family" (Gilliard, 251–252).

TOBOLSK 6/19 JANUARY

Baptism of the Lord

−12° SATURDAY

Went at 8 to Church with Nicholas, Tatiana, Anastasia & Aleksei.

Lovely bright, sunny day.

Painted & worked. Olga & Marie are up. Maria 36.1°

Lunched at 12. in Nicholas's room with Olga & Marie.

Worked & read. Nicholas read to us.

Tea at 4:30. Kolia came.

−15° rested.— −14°

8:00. Dined with Olga & Marie in my room.

Nicholas read to us.

6. S̄.

Went at 8 to Church: The Romanovs were permitted to attend Theophany (Western Epiphany) services under guard.

TOBOLSK 7/20 JANUARY

−20° SUNDAY

Bright & sunny again.

Read the service & prayers.

1:00. Lunched with Marie in Nicholas's room—painted & worked. Nicholas read to us a story of Leskov:

4:30. tea—Kolia.

Rested.

8:00. Dined with Marie in my room, she is quite well, only her face has still a rash—

Nicholas read to us, finished "Bretteur" & began "3 Portraits" by Turgenev.

Strong wind, −17°.

7. 3̄.

TOBOLSK 8/21 JANUARY

−11° MONDAY

Snowstorm, terrible wind.

9:20–10:00. Tatiana German grammar

10:00–11:00. Maria. Psalms 94–104.

11:30. got up.

12:00–1:00. Aleksei. Gospel of St. Mark, ch. 6–7 and *Meditations on the Divine Liturgy*.

1:00. We all lunched downstairs.

Painted & read.

4:30. tea—

Rested & wrote.

8:00. Dined with Aleksei in my room.

Nicholas read to us:

Getting warmer—

Mme. Syroboiarskaia No: 19

8. Й.

Tatiana German grammar: The children resumed their studies. *Meditations on the Divine Liturgy:* Work by Nikolai Gogol. *We all lunched downstairs:* When Alexandra was feeling well enough, she left her upstairs chambers to take meals with the rest of the family in the dining room. *Madame Syroboiarskaia No: 19:* From the letter: "They say that 'the family' is no longer allowed to go to church, except on the great feasts and perhaps on Lent. . . . They do not understand that there can be no celebration of Mass without a field chapel in one's home. . . . Just pretexts to show that they are in charge and can give orders. How mean that is. But so be it, I won't grumble. I remember that the Lord hears our prayers everywhere" (*Skorbnaia pamiatka*, 62–63).

TOBOLSK 9/22 JANUARY

卐 *Grandmama—1901.*

−9° TUESDAY

Wrote letters & painted.

1:00. Lunched with all.

Wrote & read.

4:45. tea—

8:00. Dined with Aleksei.

Nicholas read to us.— −2°. −4°

Marie R.B., Countess Uvarova,
Anna Vyrubova No. 1, & No. 2,
(through Anna Romanova)
p.c. Syroboiarsky No. 9.

9.

卐 *Grandmama—1901:* The anniversary of the death of Alexandra's grandmother Queen Victoria. In her diary, Alexandra noted the anniversary of a person's death with a swastika. In Sanskrit, *svastika* means "well-being." When Tatiana gave her mother the little notebook in which the diary was kept, she embroidered a swastika on the cloth cover she made for it. On settling in her room at the Ipatiev house, Alexandra inscribed a swastika on a window frame followed by the date, 17 (30) April 1918, and another swastika on the wall over the bed (Ross, 316). *Marie R.B.:* Probably Marie Ridiger-Beliaeva, wife of Major General A. A. Ridiger-Beliaev, a former officer in the Life Guards Dragoons. *Anna Vyrubova No. 1:* In 1918 Alexandra began a new numbering sequence for her letters to her friend Anna Vyrubova.

TOBOLSK 10/23 JANUARY

St. Gregory of Nyssa

−19° WEDNESDAY

Wrote letters.

10:00–11:00. Tatiana: Jesus Sirach: 22–27.

Painted.

1:00. Lunched downstairs.

Rested because of headache.

4:45. tea.

6:00–8:00. Rested.

8:00. Dined with Aleksei.

Nicholas read to us.

−22°

Aunt Olga, Tatiana.

10. Ī.

Aunt Olga: Grand Duchess Olga Konstantinovna, widow of the king of Greece.

TOBOLSK 11/24 JANUARY

−12° THURSDAY

Snowing.

9:15–10:00. Anastasia: *Fall of Roman Empire*. Pulcheria. Marcian. Attila. Honorius. Alarich. Genserich. Pope Leo. Emperor Justinian. Rise of the Papacy. 5 Roman Patriarch Constantine

Aleksei: Antioch of Jerusalem. Pope Nicholas I. Patriarch Photius. Methodius and Cyrill.

867. Council. filioque. Finished *History of the Church*.

10:00–11:00. Tatiana: German reading. "Freie Bahn" by Werner.

12:00–1:00. Olga helped me looking through my money.

1:00. Lunched downstairs.

Painted. Saw the occulist for new glasses.

4:45. tea—bezique with Olga.

One sends Isa out of the Kornilov house to-day, she has taken 2 rooms with Miss Mather & her maid in a little house.—

Rested.

8:00. Dined with Aleksei.

Nicholas read to us.—

−12°

11. ѦІ.

867. Council: At a council in 867, Patriarch Photius excommunicated Pope Nicholas I. *Filioque:* Latin, "and from the Son." A sixth-century Western addition to the Nicene Creed that was rejected by Eastern Orthodoxy. *One sends Isa out of the Kornilov house to-day:* Buksgevden was evicted by demand of the soldiers' committee. *Miss Mather:* An English friend of the deceased mother of Buksgevden. *Rested:* Alexandra wrote on this day to Colonel Syroboiarsky: "The children are sledding their hearts out on a snow mountain and taking the most amazing falls. It's a wonder they haven't broken their necks. They're all covered with bruises, but even so, this is the only distraction they have, either that or sit at the window (which I love to do very much)" (*Skorbnaia pamiatka,* 63–64).

TOBOLSK 12/25 JANUARY

Holy Martyr Tatiana

−16° FRIDAY

12:00. *Moleben* for Tatiana.

12:30. Lunched downstairs.

Worked—

4:30. tea. bezique with Olga.

Rested & wrote—

8:00. Dined downstairs with all.

Nicholas read to us. tea. −19°

12. Ы̄.

Holy Martyr Tatiana: On this day the Church commemorates Holy Martyr Tatiana of Rome. This was Grand Duchess Tatiana's name day. Moleben *for Tatiana:* A service of praise and thanksgiving in times of celebration, or one of supplication in times of need.

TOBOLSK 13/26 JANUARY

−16° SATURDAY

9:15–10:00. Tatiana: explanation of the parables.

10:00–11:00. Maria: German reading "Vineta" by E. Werner—

1:00. Lunched dowstairs.

Went out for ¾ of an hour, 12 degrees, calm, warm sun—

Tatiana read to me explanation of some of Christ's parables.

4:30. tea. bezique with Olga—

Watched the repitition of the little French play.

Rested.

7:30. dinner with Baby.

9:00. All-night Vigil.

10:30. tea—

Syroboiarsky No. 10. Mme. Zizi.

13. ГІ.

All-night Vigil: A service combining vespers and matins on the eve of a holiday.
Mme. Zizi: Yelizaveta Alekseevna Naryshkina (see glossary).

TOBOLSK 14/27 JANUARY

St. Nina of Georgia

−12° SUNDAY

11:30. *Obednitsa—*

12:30. Lunched downstairs.

Went out for an hour.

Knitted & Tatiana read to me.

4:30. tea. Glorious weather.

7:00. Theatricals.

Les Deux Timides.

Comédie Vaudeville en 1 acte par M. M. Marc—
& E. Labe.
Personnes.

Thibaudier:	Nicholas.
Jules Trimoussin	P. Gilliard.
Anatole Garadoux	Valia Dolgorukov.
Cecile: fille de Thibaudier. . . .	Anastasia.
Annette: femme de chambre . .	Tatiana.

Régisseur: P. Gilliard.
Souffleur: Gen. Tatishchev.

Played very well & amusing. Except the Suite & 2 Drs. & Kolia & Mr. Gibbs only our 4 maids looked on. Lasted 30 m:

8:00. Dined downstairs.

Nicholas read to us.

14. ΔI.

Obednitsa: Abbreviated Orthodox liturgy (see glossary). In this case, the service was held at home. The soldiers' committee decreed that the Romanovs could attend church only on the major holidays known as the Great Feasts.

TOBOLSK 15/28 JANUARY

−9° MONDAY

Anastasia has the German measles now. 36.9° & is in bed.

10:10–11:00. Maria: Psalms 104–109.

12:00–1:00. Aleksei: St. Mark 7–8 & prayers.

1:00. Lunched with Anastasia in the girls' bedroom. At 3: 37.1½°—Spent the afternoon with her—

4:45. tea. bezique with Olga. −6°

6:00. Anastasia 36.8½°

Rested & wrote.

8:00. Dined with Anastasia & Aleksei.

9:00. Anastasia: 37.4½°—

Nicholas read to us. −3°

Zina Tolstaia No. 5.

15. ЄІ҃.

TOBOLSK 16/29 JANUARY

−3° TUESDAY.

Anastasia 37.1°.

Wrote.

1:00. Lunched with Anastasia.

Went out for ¾ of an hour.

Sat with Anastasia 37.3½°. −2°

6:00. Anastasia 37.4°.

Watched the repitition of a new play.

8:00. Dined with Anastasia & Baby.

Nicholas read to us.

Knitted & bezique.

9:00. Anastasia: 37.4½°. −7°

Anna Vyrubova (Slav: through Zhuk) No. 3.

16. Ѕ҃І.

Anna Vyrubova (Slav: through Zhuk) No. 3: Alexandra wrote her third letter to Anna Vyrubova in Old Church Slavonic script and sent it through the medical orderly Zhuk, who had served in the Tsarskoe Selo infirmary.

TOBOLSK 17/30 JANUARY

−15° WEDNESDAY

Strong wind.

Anastasia 36.9°.

10:00–11:00. Tatiana: Scripture lesson. Reading.

12:00–1:00. Sat with Anastasia and

1:00. lunched with her & spent the afternoon with her—
3. Anastasia: 37.1°.

4:45. tea.

6:00. Anastasia: 36.9½°.

6:30. Aleksei: Mark 8–9. Slavonic readings.

8:00. Dined with Anastasia & Baby.

9:00. Anastasia: 36.9½°.

Nicholas read to us.—

postcard to Anna Vyrubova No. 4
through Mr. Gibbs
Syroboiarsky No. 11 V.P.
Syroboiarsky No. 12 p.c. thr. Niuta

17. 31.

Niuta: Niuta (Anna Utkina) was a maid who came voluntarily to Tobolsk in late 1917 and performed various services for the Romanovs, including posting letters.

TOBOLSK 18/31 JANUARY

−21° THURSDAY

Sunny & strong wind.

Anastasia 36.6°.

10:00–11:00. Tatiana: German reading.

12:00–1:00. Maria: Scripture lesson. Reading.

1:00. Lunched with Anastasia

at 3: 36.9°.

Spent the afternoon with her.—

4:45. tea.

6:00. Anastasia: 37.1°.

8:00. Dined with Anastasia & Baby.

9:00. Anastasia 36.8°.

Nicholas read to us. −25°

Mme. Syroboiarskaia 20

18. ЙI.

TOBOLSK 19 JANUARY/1 FEBRUARY

−19° FRIDAY

Anastasia 36.4°. Got up.

12:00. painted. Splendid sunshine.

1:00. lunched downstairs with all.

Knitted.

4:15–4:45. Aleksei: The friendship of David and Jonathan. David asks Ahimelech the priest for bread, the priest gives him the shewbread. David flees further from Saul. Hides in the cave of Adullam, near Bethlehem. David goes to Mizpeh of Moab to the king.

5:00. tea. Anastasia: 36.4°.

6:00. rested & wrote.

8:00. Dined in my room with Anastasia & Aleksei.

Nicholas read to us.

Glorious moonlights. −27°

19. ѳ҃і.

The friendship of David and Jonathan: Summary in Russian of Aleksei's Old Testament reading (1 Sam. 20–22).

TOBOLSK 20 JANUARY/2 FEBRUARY

−28° SATURDAY

9:10–10:00. Tatiana: St. Euthymius the Great—

Wisdom of Jesus Son of Sirach, 21, 27–33.

Read. knitted.

Bright, glorious sunshine.

1:00. Lunched downstairs.

Knitted—

4:30. tea.

Wrote & rested.

7:30. Dined with Aleksei.

9:00. All-night Vigil.—

very strong wind. −21°

20. К̄.

−28°: Pierre Gilliard's diary: "23° R. [Reaumur] below zero. Prince Dolgorouky and I watered the snow mountain. We carried thirty buckets of water. It was so cold that the water froze on the way from the kitchen tap to the mountain. Our buckets and the snow mountain 'steamed.' Tomorrow the children can begin tobogganing" (Gilliard, 253).

TOBOLSK 21 JANUARY/3 FEBRUARY

−23° SUNDAY

Strong wind & snowing.

11:30. *Obednitsa.*

Lunched downstairs.

Knitted. 4:30 tea.

7:30. Dined downstairs.

9:00. *A la Porte*

Comédie en 1 acte par Eugène Vercousin

Personnages:

Rolande Delauney: artiste.	Mr. Gilliard
Une Dame:	Tatiana
Balthazar:	Aleksei
Un cocher:	Aleksei

Régisseur: Pierre Gilliard

well acted—

−25°. blowing hard.

Bibi. Rita.

21. К҃А.

Rita: Lady-in-waiting Margarita Sergeevna Khitrovo (see glossary). From the letter: "Don't lose heart, my dear—the worse it gets, the nearer is God with His spiritual help. Believe in Him firmly and steadfastly. He will save our precious long-suffering homeland. . . . It's horrible, what is taking place everywhere, one's soul grieves for all of these innocent victims, but He knows best why this is necessary" (*Pis'ma,* 237–238).

TOBOLSK 22 JANUARY/4 FEBRUARY

−29° MONDAY

Bright sunshine, strong wind

10:00–11:00. Maria: scripture lesson, reading.

Wrote.

1:00. Lunched downstairs. −7° in the hall.

Wrote letters.

4:45. tea. −23°.

Rested.

8:00. Dined with Baby in my room.

Nicholas read to us.

played bezique.

Blowing a gale. −25°.

Up On the hill over 30″.

Olga Porfirievna

Olga Kolzakova: Mme. Syroboiarskaia 21 / Syroboiarsky No. 13 } B.

Mme. Zizi { Anna Vyrubova 5 (through Boris Solovyov only leaves 26th.)

22. КВ.

Olga Porfirievna: Alexandra wrote to Olga Porfirievna Grekova, who had been a nurse at the infirmary at Tsarskoe Selo. *Olga Kolzakova:* Letter to another nurse at the infirmary. *through Boris Solovyov, only leaves 26th:* Boris Nikolaevich Solovyov (see glossary) arrived in Tobolsk from Petrograd on 20 January, bringing money for the imperial family, as well as letters and other items. On 26 January Solovyov left, taking a number of Alexandra's letters.

TOBOLSK 23 JANUARY/5 FEBRUARY

−28° TUESDAY

Blowing hard:—

Wrote letters.

1:00. Lunched downstairs. 6° in the hall.

wrote.

4:45. tea in Nicholas & Baby's little dressing room as warmer there—

Rested. less wind. −25°

8:00. Dined with Aleksei.

Nicholas read to us.

To Baron Taube.

23. КГ.

Wrote letters: Alexandra wrote to Anna Vyrubova: "I can barely grip the pen [because of the cold]. . . . Little One [Aleksei] wears a jersey in the rooms, and the girls wear felt boots; I know how sad it would make you to see us. . . . You'd better burn my letters, what if they come to You and start rifling through your things? . . . Then they'll hear Your name and start persecuting You again" (*Russkaia Letopis'*, 4:216–222). *Nicholas read to us:* Works of Nikolai Leskov. *To Baron Taube:* Evidently a note of congratulations to Baron Dmitry Ferdinandovich Taube, an officer of His Imperial Majesty's Life Guards First Rifle Regiment, on his marriage to Olga Grekova (see note for the previous entry).

TOBOLSK 24 JANUARY/6 FEBRUARY

Xenia's N.D.

−19° WEDNESDAY

10:00–11:00. Tatiana: *Spiritual Readings,* and Jesus Son of Sirach 33–35.—

Wrote.

1:00. Lunched downstairs. −14°

Painted.

4:45. tea—

6:00–7:00. Aleksei: Mark 9–10. Explanation of liturgy.

8:00. Dined with Baby.

Nicholas read to us.

Anna Vyrubova 6 through Solovyov, leaves 26

24. К҃Д.

Xenia's N.D.: The name day of Nicholas's sister Grand Duchess Ksenia Aleksandrovna. *Spiritual Readings:* Evidently *Spiritual Readings,* i.e., *Complete Yearly Cycle of Brief Homilies for Each Day of the Year* (Grig. Diachenko). *Wrote:* Probably to Vyrubova's emissary Boris Solovyov, currently in Tobolsk: "Let me know what you think of our situation. Our common wish is to achieve the possibility of living tranquilly, like an ordinary family, outside politics, struggle and intrigue. Write frankly, for I will accept your letter with faith in your sincerity" (Markov, 255–256). Solovyov made encoded copies of the empress's letters and notes and burned the originals in the interests of secrecy. The imperial family was able to see Solovyov only from the windows of the Governor's House. The letters were conveyed through retainers.

TOBOLSK 25 JANUARY/7 FEBRUARY

−8° THURSDAY

9:15–10:00. Anastasia: Book of the Prophet Isaiah 1–3–

10:10–11:00. Tatiana: German grammer, dictation

12:00. Maria. Ps. 109–118.64.

1:00. Lunched downstairs

Knitted. −6°

4:45. tea.

Rested & wrote

8:00. Dined with Baby.

Nicholas read to us.—

25. К҃Е.

Rested & wrote: Boris Solovyov replied to Alexandra: "Deeply grateful for the feelings and trust expressed. The situation is on the whole very serious and could become critical, and I am certain that it will take the help of devoted friends, or a miracle, for everything to turn out all right, and for you to get your wish for a tranquil life.—Your sincerely devoted Boris" (Markov, 259).

TOBOLSK 26 JANUARY/8 FEBRUARY

−5° FRIDAY

Wrote—looked through papers with Olga.

1:00. Lunched downstairs.

Knitted & looked through accounts with Zhilik.

4:45. tea.—

Rested & wrote.

7:00. Aleksei: David spares Saul's life in the cave of En-gedi. David and Abigail. The death of Nabal. David takes Abigail to wife.

8:00. Dined with Baby.

Nicholas read to us.

Aleksei did not go out as strained the sinew behind his left knee, but no pain.—

The Com. Pankratov & his help Nikolsky have been sent out of the Kornilov house by the soldiers' committee & have nothing any longer to do with us.—

Mme. Syroboiarskaia No. 22 { B.
Syroboiarsky 14 { B.
Lili Obolenskaia; Zinochka Tolstaia

KS.

Rested & wrote: The imperial family saw Boris Solovyov that day through the window. A maid gave him a farewell note from Alexandra: "You've confirmed my fears. . . . I thank you for your sincerity and courage. Friends are either in uncertain absence or else we simply have none, and I pray tirelessly to the Lord and place all my hope in Him Alone. You speak of a miracle, but isn't it already a miracle that the Lord has sent you to us here? God keep you.—Grateful Alexandra" (Markov, 262). After making an encoded copy, Solovyov burned this note. *David spares Saul's life:* Summary in Russian of Aleksei's Old Testament reading (1 Sam. 24–25.39). *The Com. Pankratov:* A Socialist Revolutionary who had been put in charge of the imperial family in 1917 by the Provisional Government. He was therefore of dubious reliability in the eyes of pro-Bolshevik soldiers. *B.:* Possibly Boris Solovyov, indicating that he carried out all four of Alexandra's letters of this date, as well as others noted in previous entries. *Lili:* Yelizaveta Nikolaevna Obolenskaia (see glossary). *Zinochka:* Zinaida Sergeevna Tolstaia (see glossary).

TOBOLSK 27 JANUARY/9 FEBRUARY

−9° SATURDAY

9:10–10:00. Tatiana: *Spir. Readings*—Jesus Son of Sirach, 35–37.

10:10–11:00. Maria: German reading.—

Wrote. Knitted.

1:00. Lunched in Baby's room, as he spent the day in bed.—

Sat with him the afternoon embroidering—

4:30. tea.

Rested & read.

7:30. Dined with Aleksei in his room—

9:00. All-night Vigil.

К3.

TOBOLSK 28 JANUARY/10 FEBRUARY

−6° SUNDAY

11:30. *Obednitsa.* Baby up.

Lunched with Aleksei in my room—

Went out for ½ hour— −3°

Knitted & drew. Kolia came.

4:30. tea. rested.

7:30. dinner in my room with Aleksei & Kolia

9:15. *La Bête Noire.*

comédie en 1 acte par Mms. Mendel et Cordier.

Personnages:

Le Docteur Dorthez . . . . Gen. Tatishchev
Frederic Dorthez, son neveu . . . . Maria
Mme. de Bellamare, veuve . . . . Tatiana
Cyprienne, sa fille . . . . Nastenka
Maman Miette . . . . Olga
(gouvernante de la maison Dorthez.
Régisseur: P. Gilliard.

La scene se passe de nos jours à Pau dans la maison de Santé du Dr. D.—

very nicely acted—

Nicholas read to us.

КИ.

Nicholas read to us: Nicholas read from the works of Turgenev.

TOBOLSK 29 JANUARY/11 FEBRUARY

−5° MONDAY

9:05–10:00. Tatiana: *Spir. Readings.* German literature

Die Meistersänger. Hans Sachs, Hans Folg—

Das Volkslied im 14, 15. Jahrhundert. ("So viel Stern am Himmel stehen.") Satyrisches Gedicht. "Reinecke Fuchs." Das Narrenschiff von Seb. Brant." Die Narrenbeschwörung v. Th. Murner. Evangelische Kirchenlied. Martin Luther. Geistliche Lieder—37 Kirchenlieder. "Herr Gott Dich loben Wir." "Eine Feste Burg" etc. Niv. Decius P. Speratus.

10:15–11:00. Maria: *Spir. Readings*—Psalms 118.64–120.

12:10–1:00. Aleksei: Mark 10–11, N. V. Gogol's *Meditations on the Divine Liturgy.*

1:00. Lunched downstairs.

Was out over an hour—

4:45. tea.

Rested & Wrote.

8:00. Dined with Baby

Nicholas read to us Leskov.

Mme. Syroboiarskaia 23. Zina Tolstaia 6

Syroboiarsky 15.

К҃ѳ.

Syroboiarsky 15: Colonel Syroboiarsky, in Vladivostok at the time.

TOBOLSK 30 JANUARY/12 FEBRUARY

−10° TUESDAY

Baby remains in bed because he hurt his foot yesterday, scarcely slept—ached.

Sat with Aleksei—Sowed.

1:00. Lunched with Baby, played cards with him, embroidered.

4:45. tea—

played cards with Aleksei.

6:45. Rested, Tatiana read to me *Spir. Readings*.

8:00. Dined with Baby.

Nicholas read to us.

Wind howling.

Λ̄.

TOBOLSK 31 JANUARY/13 FEBRUARY

−8° WEDNESDAY

Sunny & windy. Baby slept badly.

10:00–11:00. Tatiana: *Spir. Readings:* Jesus Son of Sirach, 37–40.

Wrote. Worked.

1:00. Dined near Baby's bed again. Worked in his room.

3:45. Went out for half an hour,

Knitted.

4:45. tea.

Played cards with Aleksei.

6:45. Rested

8:00. Dined with Baby. foot ached more.

Nicholas read to us.

Sat with Baby.

λ̄ā.

TOBOLSK 1/14 FEBRUARY

−4° THURSDAY

9:30–10:00. Anastasia: Isaiah 3–5.21. Aleksei slept fr. 4 on.

10:00–11:00. Tatiana: *Spir. Readings*—German reading

12:00–1:00. Maria: Psalms 120–139,

1:00. Lunched with Baby, sat & worked in his room, played cards together.

Snowstorm all day. −2°

Many of the nicest soldiers left.

4:30. tea. Rested & read.

7:30. Dined with Aleksei.

9:15. All-night Vigil—

Tho' tomorrow is a great feast, they do not let us go to Church.—

32. ΛΒ.

1 (14) February: Nicholas's diary: "We learned that orders were received at the post office to change the [calendar] style and bring it up even with the foreign one, starting with 1 February, i.e., today would already be 14 February. There will be no end to the misunderstandings and mix-ups!" Alexandra had begun indicating dates in both old and new styles in her diary on 3 (16) January 1918; Nicholas double-dated his own diary entries from 1 (14) February through 18 (31) March, but thereafter used the old style only. *Many of the nicest soldiers left:* Gilliard's diary entry for the previous day: "The Czar tells me that the demobilisation of the army has begun. . . . The Czar seems very depressed at this prospect" (Gilliard, 253).

TOBOLSK 2/15 FEBRUARY

The Meeting of the Lord

−8° FRIDAY

11:30. *Obednitsa.*

Lunched with Aleksei.

Glorious, sunny weather, went out for ¾ of an hour—

Embroidered in Baby's room & played cards with him.

4:30. tea.

Rested & wrote.

8:00. Dined with Aleksei & Kolia.

Nicholas read to us.

Valentina Ivanovna Chebotaryova,

Marie R.B. & Mishch.,

Mme. Syroboiarskaia 24. }
Syroboiarsky 16 } Anna Romanova.

33. ΛΓ.

Meeting of the Lord: Western Feast of the Purification. *Valentina Ivanovna Chebotaryova:* Senior nurse at the infirmary in Tsarskoe Selo. *Mishch.:* Possibly Adjutant General Pavel Ivanovich Mishchenko, a Don Cossack army commander.

TOBOLSK 3/16 FEBRUARY

SS. Simeon and Anna

−18° SATURDAY ANIA'S N.D.

9:15–10:00. Tatiana: *Spir. Readings.*—Jesus, Son of Sirach: 40–43.

10:00–11:00. Maria: German reading.—Aleksei up & dressed.

Wrote & worked—

1:00. Lunched with Baby in Nicholas's room—

Went out for an hour −11° in the shade & −6° in the sun—

Embroidered.

4:30. tea.

Rested, watched repitition.

7:30. Dined with Aleksei in my room.

9:00. All-night Vigil.

Nicholas read to us & we knitted.

−18°

34. ЛД.

SS. Simeon and Anna. Ania's N.D.: The Church commemorates Saints Simeon the God-Receiver and Anna the Prophetess on this date, which was also Anna Vyrubova's name day.

TOBOLSK 4/17 FEBRUARY

卐 *Serge & I. Vladimir*

−20° SUNDAY

11:30. *Obednitsa.*

Lunched dowstairs with all.

Baby went out again & Kolia.

Went out, sunned myself on the bench −6° in the shade −11°−−14°—

Knitted.

4:30. tea in Nicholas's room as so sunny.

Rested & wrote.

7:30. Dined downstairs, Kolia too.

8:45. Tatiana Mr. Gilliard & Aleksei acted

A la Porte

for the second time—very well & then followed

Packing up.

farce in one acte by B. Gattan
Dramatis personae:
Mr. Chugwater .... Anastasia
Mrs. Chugwater ...... Marie
Luggage man .... Aleksei
Stage-manager: S. Gibbs

Awfully amusing & really well & funnily given—

Nicholas read to us. −18°

Mavra, Tatiana, Yelena—

35. л҃є.

卐 *Serge:* Anniversary of the death of Grand Duke Sergei Aleksandrovich, killed by the terrorist Kaliaev in Moscow in 1905. *I. Vladimir:* Probably a relative of the imperial family. *for the second time:* The first time had been on 21 January (3 February). *Mavra, Tatiana, Yelena:* Family of the late Grand Duke Konstantin Konstantinovich: his widow, the Grand Duchess Elizaveta Mavrikievna (Mavra); their daughter, Princess Tatiana Konstantinovna; and their relative Princess Yelena Petrovna.

TOBOLSK 5/18 FEBRUARY

−18° MONDAY

9:10–10:00. Tatiana: *Spir. Readings:* German reading

10:15–11:00. Maria: *Spir. Readings*

12:10–1:00. Aleksei: Mark 11–12. *Meditations on the Divine Liturgy.*

1:00. Lunched downstairs.

Knitted.

4:30. tea.

Rested & wrote letters.

8:00. Dined with Baby.

Nicholas read to us.

Anna Vyrubova 7. thr. Annushka

36. ΛS.

Anna Vyrubova 7. thr. Annushka. Alexandra, having just received news of the death of Vyrubova's father, sent her condolences.

TOBOLSK 6/19 FEBRUARY

−12° TUESDAY

Wrote letters. painted.

1:00. Lunched downstairs. Tatishchev appeared again after 4 days.

bad cold.

Went out for half an hour—

bright sunshine.

Knitted.

4:30. tea.

Rested & read.

8:00. Dined with Baby.

Nicholas read to us.—

Mme. T. A. 8. Marie R.B.

Aunt Olga—

37. Л҃З.

Mme. T. A. 8: Letter number eight to Anna Vyrubova; Mme. T. is probably Vyrubova's mother, Madame Taneeva.

TOBOLSK 7/20 FEBRUARY

−12° WEDNESDAY

Read.

10:10–11:00. Tatiana: *Spir. Readings:* Jesus Son of Sirach 43– to the end.—

1:00. Lunched downstairs.

Went out for an hour −5°– 6° in the sun.

4:45. tea. bezique as usual with Olga.

6:00–7:00. Aleksei. David spares Saul's life the second time. Saul inquires of the witch at Endor. The death of Saul. David anointed king. David comes to Jerusalem. David takes the stronghold, dwells in it and calls it the city of David. David plays, sings and dances before the Ark—his wife despises him.

Rested & read.

8:00. Dined with Baby.

Nicholas read to us.

38. л҃и.

David spares Saul's life: Summary in Russian of Aleksei's Old Testament reading (1 Sam. 26–2 Sam. 6.16).

TOBOLSK 8/21 FEBRUARY

−15° THURSDAY

9:15–10:00. Anastasia. Pr. Isaiah 5:27–10.

10:00–11:00. Tatiana: *Spir. Readings:* German Lit; Hans Sachs 1494 jr. Nürnberg geb:—Johann Fischart—Eulenspiegel, Faust, die Schildbürger, Der ewige Jude.—

12:00–1:00. Maria: Psalms:—to the end.

1:00. Lunched with Baby & spent the afternoon with him in Nicholas's room, reading & working.

4:45. tea.

Rested & read.

Dined with Baby.

Nicholas read to us.

39. Λ̄Θ.

TOBOLSK 9/22 FEBRUARY

−10° FRIDAY

Wrote letters. painted.

1:00. Lunched with Baby in Nicholas's room.

Worked.

Went out for half an hour, ideal weather, glorious sunshine.

4:30. Aleksei: Mark 12–13. *Meditat. on Div. Liturgy.*

5:00. tea—

Rested & wrote.

8:00. Dined with Aleksei.

Nicholas read to us.

Syroboiarsky 17. Kitty 15.

Mme. Syroboiarskaia 25 Bibi.

40. M̄.

TOBOLSK 10/23 FEBRUARY

−13° SATURDAY

9:15–10:00. Tatiana: Prophet Jeremiah 1–6—

10:10–11:00. Maria: German reading.

Wrote.

1:00. Lunched downstairs.

Went out for an hour. Baby too.

Worked.

4:30. tea. more of the nice soldiers leave to-morrow.

Looked through my money with Zhilik.

7:30. Dined with Aleksei.

Knitted.

9:00. All-night Vigil.

41. **мa҃.**

Looked through my money with Zhilik: Alexandra repeatedly records going over accounts with Zhilik (Pierre Gilliard). The Romanovs' maintenance had been abruptly curtailed and they were forced to economize (see 14 [27] February).

TOBOLSK 11/24 FEBRUARY

Sunday of the Publican and Pharisee

−11°–−4° SUNDAY

11:00. *Obednitsa.*—

12:00. Luncheon.

Went out for half an hour, watched the rifles leaving. embroidered

4:30. tea.

Rested & wrote.

7:30. Dined downstairs.

Played chicane with Trina.

Windy, bright moon.

at 9:15—

for the second time Le Fl. de John (Dec. 6.)

Le Fluide de John.

Comédie en 1 acte par M. Hannequin

Personne

Duplagné . . . . Mr. Gilliard.
John, son domestique . . . . Aleksei.
Lucien, neveu de Duplagné . . . . . Marie.
Régisseur. P. Gilliard.
In and out of a punt.
by H. V. Esmond.
Dramatis personae
Margaret . . . . Tatiana.
Hugh . . . . Mr. Gibbs.
Stage manager S. Gibbs.

very amusing & nicely acted.

42. ѦВ҃.

Went out for half an hour, watched the rifles leaving: Nicholas's diary: "We watched from the snow mountain as a whole caravan of riflemen departed on sledges." Gilliard's diary entry for 17 February (4 March): "The soldiers' committee has decided to abolish the snow mountain we have built (it was such a source of amusement to the children!) because the Czar and Czarina mounted it to watch the departure of the men of the 4th Regiment. Every day now brings fresh vexations to the Czar's family and their suite" (Gilliard, 255).

TOBOLSK 12/25 FEBRUARY

St. Alexis

−9° MONDAY ALICE'S B.D. 33.

9:15–10:00. Tatiana: Volksbücher in 16ten Jahrh.:

Kersen geb. 1488 Ulrich V. Hutten. Franz v. Lickingen.—

Burchart Waldes, Erasmus Alberus, B. Ringwald.

G. Rollenhagen ("Froschmäusele")

10:00–11:00. Maria : *Spir. Readings.*—

Wrote.

12:00–1:00. Aleksei: Mark 13–14, *Meditat. on Div. Liturgy*

1:00. Lunched downstairs

2:00–5:00. Went over accounts with Zhilik.

tea—rested, headache.

8:00. Dined with Baby.

Nicholas read to us.

43. МГ.

Alice's B.D. 33: The thirty-third birthday of Alexandra's niece Alice, Queen Victoria's great-granddaughter. *Wrote:* To Syroboiarskaia.

TOBOLSK 13/26 FEBRUARY

−11° TUESDAY

Wrote & read.

1:00. Lunched downstairs.

Looked through accounts with Zhilik.

5:00. tea.

Rested.—

8:00. Dined with Baby.

Spoke over money affairs with Valia.

Nicholas read to us.

Heard that dear old General Ivanov has been killed at Kiev & also Metropolitan Vladimir.

Syroboiarsky 18.

44. М҃Д.

General Ivanov: False reports of the murder of General I. I. Ivanov had appeared in the press. *Metropolitan Vladimir:* Metropolitan of Kiev and Galicia, Bishop Vladimir became one of the first victims of the Bolshevik terror. *Syroboiarsky 18:* Alexandra wrote: "The Germans are at Pskov. Peace will be concluded on the most horrible, disgraceful and ruinous terms for Russia. One's hair stands on end, but God will save. . . . I think that this 'infectious disease' will spread to Germany, but there it will be far more dangerous and worse. . . . The Motherland is young and will sustain this terrible disease and the whole organism will strengthen, but if everything ends this way, then in several years there will be another war. . . . I'm constantly longing to go to church, and pour my heart out there" (*Skorbnaia pamiatka*, 64–68). By "infectious disease" Alexandra meant revolution.

TOBOLSK 14/27 FEBRUARY

−11° WEDNESDAY

Read.

10:00–11:00. Tatiana: Jeremiah 6–10

Read & worked.

1:00. Lunched downstairs

Looked through accounts with Zhilik.

3:00–4:00. Went out.

Tea.

6:00. Aleksei. Gospel of the day—David wages successful wars. David comes to love Bathsheba, wife of Uriah. The prophet Nathan prophesies to David the death of David and Bathsheba's child. Amnon killed by Absalom. David flees Jerusalem with his household, ascends the Mount of Olives. Shimei curses David, casting stones at him.

8:00. Dined with Baby.

Spoke over affairs with Valia. He told all our servants to-day that we shall only receive 4000 rubles a month, 600 each of us 7 & so must part with ten of them, & live much more restrictly—& take all into our hands fr. the first of March new style (Bolshevik style).—

Nicholas read to us.

45. **МЕ҃.**

David wages successful wars: Summary in Russian of Aleksei's Old Testament reading (2 Sam. 8, 11.2–13.29, 15.16, 16.5–13). *must part with ten of them:* On 12 (25) February Alexandra wrote Syroboiarskaia: "We'll have to part with people who came here with us and have served us for a long time, but we cannot go on. So many of them will be without positions now, without work, pension, housing and maintenance. . . . All because of us . . . and we are not at fault. But one aches for them" (*Skorbnaia pamiatka*, 64).

TOBOLSK 15/28 FEBRUARY

−12° THURSDAY

9:15–10:00. Anastasia: Isaiah 10–13.

10:00–11:00. Tatiana: German reading.

12:00–1:00. Maria: Book of the Wisdom of Solomon 1–5.

1:00. Lunched downstairs.

2:30–5:00. Looked through accounts with Zhilik & payment of all the wages.

tea.

6:00–6:45. Continued with Zhilik & Tatiana

8:00. Dined with Aleksei.

Talked over affairs with Valia.

Nicholas read to us.

46. МЅ.

Nicholas read to us: Nicholas read Nikolai Leskov's *Cathedral Folk* (1872).

TOBOLSK 16 FEBRUARY/1 MARCH

−10° FRIDAY

Wrote & read.

12:00–1:00. Worked with Zhilik, Marie helped.

1:00. Lunched downstairs.

Continued with Zhilik & Tatiana.

Embroidered.

4:20–5:00. Aleksei: Mark 14–15. *On Div. Liturgy*

tea.

Rested & wrote.

8:00. Dined with Baby.

Nicholas read to us.

Heard that G. Yanushkevich was killed in the train near Gatchina.

Prince Orlov has had a stroke at Yalta!!! & that Sergeev (Crimean Cavalry Regiment) has been killed there amongst others.

Malama.

47. М҃З.

Continued with Zhilik: Gilliard's diary: "The new régime comes into force. From today butter and coffee are excluded from the table as luxuries" (Gilliard, 255). *Nicholas read to us:* Tolstoy's *Anna Karenina*. *G. Yanushkevich was killed:* Probably Nicholas's former chief of staff general Nikolai Nikolaevich Yanushkevich. *Prince Orlov:* Prince Vladimir Nikolaevich Orlov, former major general in Nicholas's suite. *Sergeev:* Alexandra received news that the Bolsheviks had routed the Crimean Cavalry Regiment, whose patron she had been. *Malama:* A letter to or from Dmitry Yakovlevich Malama, a former officer of His Imperial Majesty's Life Guards Lancers Regiment.

−4° SATURDAY

9:15–10:00. Tatiana: Jeremiah 10–16.
10:00–11:00. Maria: German reading
snowing.
embroidered.
1:00. Lunched downstairs.
Went out for half an hour.
Worked.
4:30. tea.
Rested.
7:30. Dined with Aleksei.
9:00. All-night Vigil.

48. м҃и.

TOBOLSK 18 FEBRUARY/3 MARCH

Sunday of the Prodigal Son

−2° SUNDAY

11:30. *Obednitsa—*

Lunched downstairs.

Went out for an hour.

Practised singing with the girls & Nagorny, as the choir wont sing any more.

tea.

Assisted at the repitition of the Russian play.

7:30. Dined downstairs, Kolia too.

Played kabala with Trina, at 9:15.

The Crystal Gazer

a comic sketch by Leop: Montague esq.

Dram. pers.

Miss Bessie Blank.	Maria.
The Crystal Gazer.	Mr. Gibbs.
Stage Manager.	Mr. Gibbs.

The Bear

A. Chekhov
Cast of characters
Yel. Iv. Popova . . . Olga.
Gr. St. Smirnov . . . Nicholas.
Luka . . . . Maria.

49. М҃Ѳ.

Practised singing: Alexandra, her daughters, and their retainers formed a choir for worship services in the Governor's House. *Nagorny:* Aleksei's personal caretaker (see glossary).

TOBOLSK 19 FEBRUARY/4 MARCH

Week of Meatfare

−6° MONDAY

9:15–10:00. Tatiana: German reading.

10:00–11:00. Maria: Wisdom of Solomon 5–7.

12:00–1:00. Aleksei: Mark 15–to the end.—
Meditat. on Div. Liturgy

1:00. Lunched downstairs. Heard that Felix's ~~has~~ cousin been killed at Kiev & Rodz's son too!!!

Looked through accounts with Zhilik & Tatiana—

Wrote & worked.

4:45. tea.

Rested.

8:00. Dined with Baby.

Nicholas read to us.

Syroboiarsky No. 19, Xenia, Countess Ye. P. Kleinmikhel, Mme. Syroboiarskaia 26

50. Н̄.

Week of Meatfare: In Orthodoxy, the last week before the Great Fast (Western Lent) during which meat can be eaten. *Felix's cousin:* Felix is Prince Feliks Feliksovich Yusupov, instigator of the murder of Rasputin (see glossary). Alexandra at first recorded a false report that Yusupov himself had been killed at Kiev, then corrected her entry to read that his cousin was killed. (Yusupov mentions no relative being killed on this date in his memoirs.) *Rodz's son:* Rodz is Alexandra's shorthand for Mikhail Vladimirovich Rodzianko. His son Georgy Mikhailovich Rodzianko, a captain in the Life Guards Preobrazhensky Regiment, was shot on 26 January (18 February) 1918.

TOBOLSK   20 FEBRUARY/5 MARCH

−6° TUESDAY

Strong wind, snow & sun—

Read.

1:00. Lunched downstairs.

Sowed.

4:45. tea.

practised our singing for church.

Rested.

8:00. Dined with Baby.

Nicholas read to us.

51. **N̄A.**

TOBOLSK 21 FEBRUARY/6 MARCH

−15° WEDNESDAY

10:00–11:00. Tatiana: Jeremiah 16–24.

Wrote. Cold & sunny.

1:00. Lunched downstairs.

Worked & wrote sang.

4:45. tea.

6:15–7:00. Aleksei: David crosses the Jordan with his people. The death of Absalom. Joab. Battles against the Philistines. Pestilence in Jerusalem. The prophet Gad. King David orders his and Bathsheba's son Solomon to be proclaimed and anointed. David gives Solomon all materials and plans for the Temple which he charges him to build. David praises God. David dies—reigned forty years.

Psalms.—Rested.

8:00. Dined with Baby.

Nicholas read to us.

52. **NB.**

David crosses the Jordan: Summary in Russian of Aleksei's Old Testament reading (2 Sam. 17.22–18, 20–22, 24.11–25; 1 Kings 1–2.11).

TOBOLSK 22 FEBRUARY/7 MARCH

−7° THURSDAY

9:15–10:00. Anastasia: Psalms 13–20.

10:00–11:00. Tatiana: German reading.

12:00–1:00. Maria: Wisdom of Solomon 7–12—

Lunched downstairs—

Zhilik. embroidered—

4:30. tea. short snowstorm.

Practised our singing, again the regent did not come—

Rested—

8:00. Dined with Baby.

Nicholas read to us.

heard that my old Kondratiev died—

53. **Ѓ҃Г**.

the regent: Person who leads singing. *my old Kondratiev:* Vladimir Aleksandrovich Kondratiev, gentleman-in-waiting of the imperial court.

AT 10 'CLOCK

TOBOLSK 23 FEBRUARY/8 MARCH

−4° 4° SUN FRIDAY

9:15–10:00. Aleksei: Luke 1–2—

copied out.

1:00. Lunched downstairs. Sat on the balkony more than an hour.

Worked.

4:45. tea.

Rested & read.

8:00. Dined with Baby.

Nicholas read to us.

54. НД.

TOBOLSK 24 FEBRUARY/9 MARCH

Forefathers Saturday

−5° SATURDAY

9:15–10:00. Tatiana: Jeremiah 24–31:13.

10:15–1:00. Maria: German reading.

wrote.

1:00. Lunched downstairs.

Sat ¾ of an hour on balkony.

Worked.

4:30. tea—

Rested.

7:30. Dined with Aleksei.

9:00. All-night Vigil, choir sings now again:

Heard that charming Gubaryov (Crimean Cavalry Regiment) has been killed.

The choir of 4 women, a tenor & the regent sing now gratis.

55. NG.

that charming Gubaryov: Captain of the Cavalry treated at Alexandra's infirmary in Tsarskoe Selo, who perished on 1 January 1918 in Simferopol as the regiment was being routed by Sevastopol sailors.

TOBOLSK 25 FEBRUARY/10 MARCH

−17° SUNDAY

11:30. *Obednitsa.*

Lunched alone upstairs ♡.

Wrote.

4:30. tea.

Wrote, rested.

8:00. Dined alone—

Played chicane with Trina.

9:30.— For the second time:

Packing up.

Mr. Chugwater — Anastasia

Mrs. Chugwater — Maria

Luggageman — Aleksei

very gaily acted.

Nicholas read to us.

56. NS.

♡: Apparently Alexandra's heart was causing her pain, and she could not join the family in the downstairs dining room.

TOBOLSK 26 FEBRUARY/11 MARCH

Week of Cheesefare

−16° −10° MONDAY *Maslenitsa*

Nicholas's father's B.D.

9:00–10:00. Tatiana: *Spir. Readings.*

10:00–11:00. Maria: Wisdom of Solomon 12–17.

12:00–1:00. Aleksei: Luke 2–4. *Meditat. on Div. Liturgy.*

1:00. Lunched with Baby.

Spent the afternoon (writing) with him, as he hurt his toe & so must keep the foot up or lie on the floor— snowed.

4:45. tea.

Rested & wrote.

8:00. Dined with Aleksei.

Nicholas read to us.

Syroboiarsky No. 20.

57. **Н͞З.**

Maslenitsa: From *maslo* (butter), the holiday also known as the Week of Cheesefare, a weeklong pre-Lenten celebration in Slavic countries during which eating meat is forbidden but eating dairy products and eggs is permitted. *Nicholas's father's B.D.:* The birthday of Emperor Alexander III.

TOBOLSK 27 FEBRUARY/12 MARCH

TUESDAY

Wrote.

1:00. Lunched with Baby.

Wrote—Baby looked at newspapers.

4:45. tea.

Rested & wrote.

8:00. Dined with Aleksei.

Nicholas read to us.

58. Ñи.

TOBOLSK 28 FEBRUARY/13 MARCH

卐 *Papa 26th anniversary*

−17° WEDNESDAY

10:00–11:00. Tatiana: *Spir. Readings.* Jeremiah 31:13—to the end.

Wrote.

1:00. Lunched with Baby.

Spent the afternoon as yesterday.

4:45. tea.

6:00–7:00. Aleksei: Solomon asks God for wisdom. Solomon's judgment. Solomon's proverbs. The building of the Temple (7 years). The queen of Sheba visits Solomon. Solomon is drawn to idolatry, the prophet Ahijah. Solomon seeks to kill Jeroboam, but Jeroboam escapes. Solomon dies, reigned 40 yrs. His son Rehoboam is made king.

Zina Tolstaia 7.

59. N◈.

卐 *Papa 26th anniversary:* Anniversary of the death of Alexandra's father, Grand Duke Louis IV of Hesse. *Solomon asks God for wisdom:* Summary in Russian of Aleksei's Old Testament reading (1 Kings 3–7, 10–12).

TOBOLSK 1/14 MARCH

卐 Alexander II

−17° THURSDAY

9:20–10:00. Anastasia: Isaiah 20–26.

12:00–1:00. Maria: Wisdom of Solomon: 17– to the end—

1:00. Lunched with Baby.

2:00. *Panikhida*—

Painted.

4:45. Tea.

6:00–8:00. Rested & wrote—

8:00. Dined with Aleksei.

Nicholas read to us. −20°

Anna Vyrubova 9, 10 {post

Nini Voeikova, Emma Frederiks, Lili Den 3, Aunt Olga through Boris Solovyov

60. ℨ.

卐 Alexander II: Thirty-seventh anniversary of the assassination of Emperor Alexander II (see glossary). *Panikhida:* A memorial service, held in the Governor's House for Alexander II. *Nini Voeikova:* Yevgenia Vladimirovna Voeikova, daughter of Count Boris Vladimirovich Frederiks, minister of the imperial court and domains (see glossary). *Emma Frederiks:* Emma Vladimirovna Frederiks, sister of Nini Voeikova (see glossary).

TOBOLSK 2/15 MARCH

⚡ David Grabovoi 1915

−20° FRIDAY

Wrote letters.

1:00. Lunched with Baby. He went out to-day again.

Painted & wrote—

4:45. tea.

Rested & wrote—

Anniversary of Nicholas's abdication!!!

8:00. Dined with Aleksei.

Nicholas read to us.

61. ѯа҃.

⚡ David Grabovoi: An officer of the 14th Georgian Regiment (of which Aleksei was the patron) who died on this date in 1915 at the Tsarskoe Selo infirmary. *Wrote letters:* Alexandra may have written some of the letters whose addressees are listed in the previous entry. The arrow suggests that this group of letters was actually sent out on 2 (15) March.

TOBOLSK 3/16 MARCH

−12° SATURDAY

Wrote.

1:00. Lunched with Baby.

Looked through accounts with Zhilik.

wrote—

4:30. tea.

Rested.

7:30. Dined with Aleksei

9:00. All-night Vigil.

p.c. Syroboiarsky 21, Zina Tolstaia 8.
Garan

62. ѯ҃в.

Wrote: Alexandra wrote to Anna Vyrubova: "What a nightmare, that the Germans are supposed to save everyone and establish order. What could be worse and more degrading than that? We accept order given with one hand, while with the other they're taking everything away. God save and help Russia! Nothing but disgrace and horror" (*Russkaia Letopis'*, 4:226).

TOBOLSK 4/17 MARCH

Forgiveness Sunday

SUNDAY

Wrote.

11:30. *Obednitsa*. Lunched with Baby.

Looked through accounts with Zhilik.

Wrote.

4:30. tea.

Practised singing.

8:00. Dined with Aleksei.

Nicholas read to us.

63. ѮГ.

Forgiveness Sunday: Orthodox holiday falling on the last day of Maslenitsa, the eve of Great Lent, when believers ask one another's forgiveness for past offenses.

TOBOLSK 5/18 MARCH

1st week of Great Lent

−8° 8° SUN MONDAY

9:00. Service, Olga, Tatiana, Maria, Anastasia & I sang with the new Deacon—not well of course as had no rehearsal, he remained after service still to try through some things for the evening service.

Wrote—

1:00. Lunched with Baby.

Sat with Nastinka on the balkony in the sun.

4:30. tea—

Wrote.

7:00. Service—

8:00. Dined with Aleksei.

Spent the evening without suite. Nicholas read the life of St. Nicholas.

Earlier to bed.

Anna Vyrubova 11

64: ѯ҃д.

1st week of Great Lent: Gilliard's diary: "During the first week of Lent, the family will perform its devotions as usual" (Gilliard, 257). *Anna Vyrubova 11:* From the letter: "Don't know anything new—my heart is hurting, but there is a brightness in my soul, I feel the closeness of the Heavenly Creator, Who in His mercy never abandons His own. But the things happening in Moscow!! God help us!" (*Russkaia Letopis'*, 4:227).

TOBOLSK 6/19 MARCH

TUESDAY

9:00. Service, afterwards ½ h. choir rehearsal.

Tatiana 12:15–1:00. *Spirit. Readings.*

1:00. Luncheon with Baby.

Wrote & painted & read.

practised

4:45. tea.

Rested.

7:00. Evening service (went better)

8:00. Dined with Baby.

Worked, early to bed.

Mme. Syroboiarskaia 27.
Syroboiarsky 22.

65. З҃Є.

Mme. Syroboiarskaia 27: Alexandra wrote Syroboiarskaia about the Treaty of Brest-Litovsk, just signed with the Germans, which had driven both her and Nicholas to despair: "What kind of times are these? What next? An utterly disgraceful peace. It's simply horrible, what they've done in a single year. All they've done is destroy everything. A degrading peace. But the Lord is supreme, and maybe where people are powerless He will do something about things. Something special is coming that will save. Being under the German yoke, you know, is worse than the Tartars. No, the Lord won't permit such an injustice" (*Skorbnaia pamiatka*, 63).

TOBOLSK 7/20 MARCH

*Orchie's B.D. Grosspapa*卐
Toddie's 29th B.D.

−6° WEDNESDAY

8:00. Presanctified Mass at last again in Church—sunshine.

Painted, practised alone.

12:00. Lunched with Aleksei.

Painted—Tatiana read *Spir. Readings* to me.

4:30. tea.

Rested.

7:00. Service, sang better—

8:00. Dined with Baby.

Worked, early to bed.

66. ѯ҃ѕ.

Orchie's B.D.: Birthday of Mary Anne Orchard, Alexandra's childhood nurse, deceased. *Grosspapa*卐: The anniversary of the death of Alexandra's paternal grandfather, Prince Carl of Hesse-Darmstadt. *Toddie's 29th B.D.:* Birthday of Prince Waldemar-Wilhelm of Prussia, Alexandra's nephew. *Presanctified:* Liturgy of the Presanctified Gifts (see glossary). *Mass:* Alexandra used the English term *mass* and the Russian *obednia* interchangeably. *again in Church:* The evening before, Alexandra wrote to Madame Syroboiarskaia: "We've been permitted to be in church on Wednesday, Friday and Saturday mornings (we're taking communion after two months), this will be such a joy and a consolation. One feels so strongly drawn there during such a difficult time. Praying at home is not the same thing at all—in the room where we sit, where the piano is and where we've put on plays" (*Skorbnaia pamiatka*, 63).

TOBOLSK 8/21 MARCH

*Grossmama*卐

−6° THURSDAY

9:00. Service.
Pract: with the deacon—
painted.
1:00. Lunched with Baby—
painted, sang a little, wrote.
4:30. tea. practised—
rested—
7:00. Service.
8:00. Dined with Aleksei.
Nicholas read to us life of St. Nikolai—

Syroboiarsky 23.

67. 33.

*Grossmama*卐: The anniversary of the death of Alexandra's grandmother Princess Elizabeth of Prussia.

TOBOLSK 9/22 MARCH

−4° FRIDAY

8:00. Presanctified Mass in Church.

Had to walk all way as path too bad for chair.

Rested & read.

12:00. Lunched with Baby.

Painted, practised singing.

rested.

4:15. tea.

Rested.

7:00. Dined with Aleksei.

8:00. Service we sang.—

9:15–12:00. Confession, we 7, Nastinka, Valia, Tatishchev, Liza & 11 of our men. children began & we at the end.

Sat 11:15.—

68. ѯи҃.

9 (22) March: Nicholas's diary: "Today is the anniversary of my arrival in Tsarskoe Selo and my confinement with the family in Alexandrovsky Palace. One can't help recalling this difficult year! And what still awaits us ahead? All is in God's hands! We place all our hope in Him alone. At 8:00, we went to Mass. We spent the day as always." *Confession:* After vespers the imperial family, their suite, and servants made their confessions to the priest. *Liza:* Yelizaveta Nikolaevna Ersberg, the grand duchesses' chambermaid who for many years was assistant to the nanny Aleksandra Teglyova.

TOBOLSK 10/23 MARCH

−4° SATURDAY

7:30. Mass & holy Communion—walked there & back fr. Church—

choir sang beautifully.

Painted & read.

12:00. Lunched with Baby.

1:00. Painted & worked.

4:30. tea.

Rested.

7:30. Dined with Aleksei.

8:45. Evening service, small choir.

Suite stayed for tea, & at
11:30. Separated.—

69. ѯ҃ѳ.

Evening service, small choir: Service was celebrated at home and without choristers; Alexandra and her daughters sang under the deacon's direction.

TOBOLSK 11/24 MARCH

SUNDAY

Glorious sunshine, several degrees of warmth in the sun & zero in the shade.

11:30. *Obednitsa*/choir

Lunched with Baby.

Painted.

Sat on the balkony.

4:30. tea.

Rested.

8:00. Dined with Aleksei.

Nicholas read to us all—

70. ō.

TOBOLSK 12/25 MARCH

2d week of Great Lent

MONDAY

9:00–10:00. Tatiana: *Spir. Readings.*

10:00–11:00. Maria: *The Ray of Spirit.*

painted.

12:00–1:00. Aleksei: Luke 4, *Meditat. on Div. Liturgy.*

1:00. Lunched with Baby.

Sat on the balkony—

Saw my ex-Crimean Markov pass & Shtein too.—

4:30. tea.

5:30–7:30. Looked through money with Tatiana & Zhilik.

8:00. Dined with Aleksei.

Nicholas read to us.

Mme. Syroboiarskaia No: 28.

70. ō.

Saw my ex-Crimean Markov pass: Sergei Markov (see glossary) brought various items and letters from Anna Vyrubova and others to Tobolsk. The previous evening Alexandra had passed him a large cigarette-holder, other souvenirs, and a note. Markov wrote that on this date he caught sight of the imperial family gathered in the second-floor windows of the Governor's House as he passed on the street. He lingered, painstakingly fixed a cigarette to his cigarette-holder, and on lighting the cigarette saw Alexandra nod to him cautiously. He returned the Romanovs' gaze as long as he could, silently paying his respects to the family while attempting to suppress his sobs (Markov, 222–223). *Shtein too:* Vladimir Nikolaevich Shtein, second vice-governor of Mogilyov during Nicholas's tenure at Stavka (headquarters), brought 250,000 rubles for the imperial family from a monarchist organization. *Mme. Syroboiarskaia No: 28:* Alexandra wrote: "Again began to sketch prayers and even little icons on paper out of gratitude to those who are generously spoiling us here these days. Giving us jams, pirozhki, tea biscuits and so on, coffee, tea. Terribly touching how people do this for one on the quiet" (*Skorbnaia pamiatka*, 67).

TOBOLSK 13/26 MARCH

3° TUESDAY

Wrote & read.

1:00. Lunched with Baby.

Sat on the balkony, glorious sunshine.

Wrote.

4:30. tea—

Rested & read.

8:00. Dined with Aleksei.

Nicholas read to us.—

Anna Vyrubova 12.

Nicholas read to us: Turgenev's *Spring Torrents*. *Anna Vyrubova 12:* From the letter: "Tell little M. [Markov] that his patron was very glad to see him. . . . 26 years since I buried my own father. . . . and I thank God that he's not alive today. . . . [W]e shall share [Christ's sufferings] with Him, enduring without protest all the sufferings God has sent down to us. Why ought we not to suffer, if He, innocent and sinless, freely suffered? We are atoning for all our age-old sins; we are washing away in blood all the blemishes that have polluted our souls" (*Russkaia Letopis'*, 4:227–230).

TOBOLSK 14/27 MARCH

Feast of the Fyodorovskaia Most-Holy Mother of God

WEDNESDAY

Wrote. & read.

10:00–11:00. Tatiana: Jeremiah's lament, Baruch.—

Wrote.

1:00. Lunched with Baby.

copied 2° shade

4:30. tea.

6:00–7:00. Aleksei: Division of Solomon's kingdom. Rehoboam and Jeroboam. Prophecies of the man of God. Prophet. Idolatry. Death of Jeroboam's child. " in Israel:— Shishak king of Egypt comes to Jerusalem and takes away all its treasures. Death of Rehoboam. His son Abijam made king. Abijam's war with Jeroboam. Abijam and Jeroboam die. Jeroboam succeeded by his son Nadab, Asa by Abijam. Asa burns the idols. The prophet Azariah.—

Tatiana read the Akathist to the Fyodorovskaia Mother of God to me.

8:00. Dined with Baby.

Nicholas read to us. −4°

14 (27) March: Nicholas's diary: "The armed detachment here was disbanded when soldiers of all classes were discharged." Gilliard's diary: "[Her] Majesty . . . tells me [she] has reason to believe that there are among [the men of the newly arrived Omsk guard detachment] many officers who have enlisted in the ranks; [she] also asserts, without telling me definitely the source of [her] information, that there are three hundred officers at Tiumen" (Gilliard, 257–258). The imperial family could expect the support and sympathy of former officers, whereas most soldiers were against them. *Division of Solomon's kingdom:* Summary in Russian of Aleksei's Old Testament reading (1 Kings 12, 14.17–15.13; 2 Chron. 9–15). *Akathist:* A hymn of praise often glorifying the Mother of God, sung standing (Pokrovskii, 7–8). *Feodorovskaia Mother of God:* The patronal icon of the Romanov dynasty.

TOBOLSK 15/28 MARCH

−10° THURSDAY

9:00–10:00. Anastasia: Isaiah 26–29.

10:00–11:00. Tatiana. Johann Arnd. "Wahres Christenthum"—Periode der Nachahmung. Martin Opitz, 1539–1639. Paul Fleming. Andreas Gryphius. Friedrich von Logan. (Epigramm) Simon Dach. (Annchen von Tharau). Evangel: Kirchenlied im 1006. 1676. 17. Jahrh: Paul Gerhardt (Wach auf mein Herz & Singe: "O Haupt voll Blut & Wunden"—"Befiehl du deine Wege.") Luise Henriette (17. des Kurf. von Brand:) Jesus meine Zuversicht. Georg Neumark. Wer nur den lieben Gott lässt walten. Rinkart Nun danket alle Gott.—Die 2te schlesiche Schule: Hoffmann v. Hoffmannswaldau Lohenstein. Chr. Günther. An. Gryphius. Wernicke. Frh. v. Canitz (Hofpoet Konig fr. t) Chr. Weise Pros. Satire & d. Roman des 17. J. Chr. V. Grimmelshausen (D. Simplizissimus) Haller & Hagedorn. Gottsched. Bodmer. Leipziger Bund.

—German reading.

12:00–1:00. Maria: Wisdom of Jesus Son of Sirach, 1–6.

1:00. Lunched with Baby. He does not go out as has a cough, red to him Leikin's *Where the Oranges Ripen.*

painted & worked.

4:30. tea. rested.

8:00. Dined with Baby.

Nicholas read to us.

Syroboiarsky 24.

Leikin's Where the Oranges Ripen: Nikolai Aleksandrovich Leikin, Russian humorist.

TOBOLSK 16/29 MARCH

−8° FRIDAY

Snowing hard.

9:06–10:00. Aleksei. Luke 5–7 v. 28.

Wrote.

1:00. Lunched with Aleksei.

painted, read & wrote. Read to Baby.

4:00–4:12. *Meditat. on Div. Liturgy*

4:30. tea.

Rested & read.

8:00. Dined with Baby.

Nicholas read aloud.

snowstorm all day.

Zina Tolstaia 9.

TOBOLSK 17/30 MARCH

−11° SATURDAY

Sunshine & windy Anniv: Ct. Hendr: 卐

9:00–10:00. Tatiana: Ezekiel 1–14.

10:00–11:00. Maria: German reading.

12:15–1:00. Nicholas read to me & I worked.

1:00. Lunched with Aleksei,

Worked & read. Sunshine,

4:30. tea.

Rested & read.

7:30. Dined with Baby.

9:00. All-night Vigil.

Anniv: Ct. Hendr: 卐: Probably the anniversary of the death of Count Vasily Aleksandrovich Hendrikov (in Russian, Gendrikov), father of Alexandra's lady-in-waiting Countess Anastasia Vasilievna Gendrikova (Nastenka).

TOBOLSK 18/31 MARCH

SUNDAY

Snowing again.

11:30. *Obednitsa.*

12:30. Lunched with Aleksei.

Worked, painted, Kolia came.

4:30. tea.

Rested & read.

8:00. Dined with Baby & Kolia.

Nicholas read to us.

77. о҃з.

TOBOLSK 19 MARCH/1 APRIL

3d week of Great Lent

MONDAY

11° in the sun at 9. −1° in the shade.

9:00–10:00. Tatiana: *Spir. Readings:*

10:00–11:00. Maria: Wisdom of J. Son of Sirach 6–11.

12:00–1:00. Aleksei: Luke 7:28–9.

1:00. Lunched with Baby.

Sat for an hour on the balkony.

embroidered—Baby went out again.

4:30. tea.

Tried our singing a little.

Rested, wrote & read.

8:00. Dined with Aleksei.

Nicholas read to us.

Zina Tolstaia 10.

3° TUESDAY

Wrote, read & worked.

1:00. Lunched with Baby.

Sat whole afternoon knitting on balkony 20° in the sun, in thin blouse & silk jacket.

4:30. tea. Looked through accounts with Zhilik.

Rested & read.

8:00. Dined with Baby.

Nicholas read to us.

Mme. Syroboiarskaia 29, Mme. Zizi Naryshkina, Emma Frederiks, Anna Vyrubova 13.

Emma Frederiks: Alexandra wrote: "The Bolsheviks have come, but nothing's happened" (Alfer'ev, 323). *Anna Vyrubova 13:* She wrote to Vyrubova: "Boris [Solovyov] has been arrested: this is bad, but they did not shoot him—he knew this would happen. We have Bolsheviks in town—it's all right, don't worry. The Lord is everywhere and will work a miracle" (*Russkaia Letopis'*, 4:230–232).

TOBOLSK 21 MARCH/3 APRIL

WEDNESDAY

Read. 1° in the shade at 7.

10:00–11:00. Tatiana: Ezekiel 14—

Daniel 1–5

Sat on the balkony & then worked.

1:00. Lunched with Aleksei.

Sat on the balkony writing,

4:30. tea.

6:30–7:00. Aleksei: Hanani the seer. The death of Asa, his son Jehoshaphat succeeds him.—King Ahab—The building of Jericho. The prophet Elijah. The woman of Zarephath feeds him and he resurrects her son. Elijah and the prophets of Baal make a sacrifice. Elijah orders the priests of Baal slain. Elijah makes Elisha his disciple. Elijah's vision on Mount Horeb. The death of Ahab; and Jezebel eaten by dogs.

8:00. Dined with Baby.

Said goodbye to 3 of our men who left us a month ago, but now go home.

Nicholas read to us.

A year to-day Anna Vyrubova & Lili Den were taken away fr. Tsarskoe Selo.

Syroboiarsky 25.

80 П̄.

Hanani the seer: Summary in Russian of Aleksei's Old Testament reading (1 Kings 15–22; 2 Chron. 16–22).

TOBOLSK 22 MARCH/4 APRIL

4° THURSDAY

9:10–10:00. Anastasia: Isaiah 29–32.

10:00–11:00. Tatiana; German reading & I embroidered.

12:20–1:00. Maria: Wisdom of J. Son of Sirach 11–18.

1:00. Lunched with Aleksei.

Sat on the balkony, cooler, less sun.

Embroidered. read.

4:30. tea. rained.

Rested & wrote & read.

8:00. Dined with Baby.

Nicholas read to us.

Mme. Syroboiarskaia 30.

81. **ПА.**

22 *March (4 April):* Nicholas's diary: "This morning we could hear the Tiumen Bolshevik bandits leaving Tobolsk in fifteen troikas with sleighbells, whistling and whooping. The Omsk detachment ran them out of town!"

TOBOLSK 23 MARCH/5 APRIL

Victoria's B.D. Sandro's B.D.

6° WITHOUT SUN FRIDAY

Worked & read.

1:00. Lunched with Baby.

Lovely weather, sat on balkony.

Looked through our money with Zhilik.

read.

4:30. tea.

Rested & read.

7:00–7:45. Aleksei: Luke 9–9.38.

8:00. Dined with Baby.

Nicholas read to us.

Victoria's B.D.: Birthday of Alexandra's oldest sister, Victoria, wife of Prince Louis of Battenberg. *Sandro's B.D.:* Possibly Grand Duke Aleksandr Mikhailovich (see glossary).

TOBOLSK 24 MARCH/6 APRIL

7° SHADE AT 8 SATURDAY

9:00–10:00. Tatiana: Daniel 5–8

Worked, wrote & read.

1:00. Lunched with Baby.

Sat on the balkony til 4.

Read.

4:30. tea.

Rested & read.

8:00. Dined with Baby.

9:45. All-night Vigil (Veneration of the Cross) three singers & Regent. Said they can't sing tomorrow before 1:30 so we shall have to sing without having practised.—

Mme. Syroboiarskaia 30.

All-night Vigil: A service on the eve of the Great Feast of the Annunciation of the Most-holy Theotokos and Ever-Virgin Mary. *Mme. Syroboiarskaia 30:* Alexandra already noted "Mme. Syroboiarskaia 30" in her entry for 22 March (4 April) but the notation on that date is very faint—possibly an erasure. The later notation is bold and dark.

TOBOLSK 25 MARCH/7 APRIL

Veneration of the Cross
The Annunciation

SUNDAY XENIA'S B.D. VICKY'S B.D.

8:00. *Obednitsa,* we sang.

Read the whole morning.

12:00. Luncheon with Baby.

Read & sat ½ hour on balkony, fresher, had snowed wee bit in the morning.

4:30. tea, Kolia too.

Rested.

8:00. Dined with Aleksei & Kolia.

Nicholas read to us.

Xenia's B.D.: Probably the birthday of Nicholas's sister Grand Duchess Ksenia Aleksandrovna. *Obednitsa, we sang:* Nicholas's diary: "Again Alix and our daughters sang without any warm-up." Nicholas addressed his wife by her German name, Alix, which corresponds to the English Alice (her mother's name). Alexandra Fyodorovna was the Russian name she took upon converting to Orthodoxy on 22 October 1894.

TOBOLSK 26 MARCH/8 APRIL

4th Week of Great Lent

2° MONDAY

9:20–10:00. Tatiana: *Spirit. Readings—*

10:00–11:00. Maria: " " and St. John Chrysostom.

Snowed a little.

12:15–1:00. Aleksei: Luke 9:38—*Meditat. on Div. Liturgy.*

1:00. Lunched with Aleksei.

Painted & wrote.

4:30. tea.

Read & rested. −3°

8:00. Dined with Baby.

Nicholas read to us. (protocols of the freemasons.)—

Mme. Syroboiarskaia 26. Zina Tolstaia 11.

protocols of the freemasons: Nicholas wrote in his diary the next day: "Yesterday I started to read aloud Nilus's book on the Antichrist, to which have been added the 'protocols' of the Jews and Masons—very timely reading matter." Nicholas evidently read Sergei Nilus's *Velikoe v malom i Antikhrist, kak blizkaia politicheskaia vozmozhnost': Zapiski pravoslavnogo* (The great in the small and the Antichrist as an imminent political possibility: Notes of an Orthodox believer) (2d ed., Tsarskoe Selo, 1905), which included the so-called *Protocols of the Elders of Zion.* The White Army investigators found the book in the Ipatiev house after the family was killed. Nilus claimed that these were the protocols of a Zionist organization bent on destroying civilization and creating a worldwide Jewish state. In fact, the *Protocols* had been fabricated by the tsarist secret police.

TOBOLSK 27 MARCH/9 APRIL

−7° TUESDAY

Sunshine. Read & wrote & embroidered.

1:00. Lunched with Aleksei.

Sat a little on the balkony.

embroidered.

4:30. tea.

Rested, wrote

8:00. Dined with Aleksei.

Nicholas read to us.

Mme. Syroboiarskaia 31.

27 March (9 April): Gilliard's diary: "The Bolshevik commissary, who has come with the detachment from Omsk, has insisted on being allowed to inspect the house. The soldiers of our guard have refused permission. Colonel Kobylinsky is very uneasy and fears a conflict. Precautionary measures; patrols, sentries doubled. A very disturbed night" (Gilliard, 258). Colonel Yevgeny Stepanovich Kobylinsky (see glossary) was commandant of the Governor's House.

TOBOLSK 28 MARCH/10 APRIL

−10° −8° WEDNESDAY

With the children & Tutels sowed up my jewels.

1:00. Lunched with Baby.

Sowed again.

Lovely sunny weather.

Sat out ¼ of an hour—then was asked to go in again.

embroidered.

4:30. tea.

Rested.

6:30–7:00. Aleksei: Luke 11:29.

8:00. Dined with Baby.

Nicholas read to us.

With the children & Tutels sowed up my jewels: Alexandra, disturbed by the new situation, decided to protect some of her jewels by sewing them into cloth-covered buttons, hats, belts, corsets, etc. Tutels was Alexandra's pet name for one of her personal maids, Maria Gustavovna Tutelberg. *Sat out ¼ of an hour—then was asked to go in again:* Nicholas's diary: "Yesterday there was unrest in our detachment due to rumors about the arrival of more Red Guards from Yekaterinburg. By nightfall the guard had been doubled, the patrols reinforced, and sentries posted in the street. There was talk of some supposed danger for us in this house and the need to move to the protopriest's house on the hill. . . . They even asked Alix not to sit on the balcony for three days!"

TOBOLSK 29 MARCH/11 APRIL

−4° THURSDAY

9:30–10:00. Aleksei: Isaiah 32–34.

10:15–11:00. Tatiana: *Spir. Readings.* & German reading.

Wrote—& embroidered.

1:00. Lunched with Aleksei.

Painted & worked.

4:30. tea.

Rested.

8:00. Dined with Baby.

Nicholas read to us.

29 *March (11 April):* Nicholas's diary: "During our morning walk we saw the 'Extraordinary Commissar' Demianov, who . . . . accompanied by the commandant and riflemen, made an inspection tour of the guards' accommodations and the garden." Demianov (Dementiev) commanded the Red Guard detachment from Omsk that had arrived in Tobolsk on 26 March to oversee the guarding of the imperial family.

TOBOLSK 30 MARCH/12 APRIL

−1° FRIDAY

Bright sunshine. Baby stays in bed as fr. coughing so hard has a slight hemorrhage in the abdom.

Read & copied.

12:00–1:00. Aleksei: Luke 11:29–13. *Meditat. on Div. Liturgy.*

1:00. Lunched with Baby in his room. Kobylinsky gave us over the order fr. Moscow that we have to put up Trina, Nastenka, Tatishchev, Valia, Mr. Gibbs in our house with their maids, so great fuss changing rooms, having partition put upon the entrance.

Embroidered & ran about & sat with Baby.

4:30. tea, went down again.

6:30. rested.

8:00. Dined with Baby. pains strong.

Sat with him.

The rest only came up for tea at 11 as were arranging their rooms downstairs.

Trina & two maids, Nastenka & her old general sleep here already to-night.—

Syroboiarsky 27.

Kobylinsky gave us over the order fr. Moscow: A soldier sent to Moscow by the soldiers of the guard detachment returned with a paper from the Central Executive Committee stating that Tatishchev, Dolgorukov, Gendrikova, and Shneider were to be considered under arrest. *Nastenka & her old general:* Gendrikova and General Tatishchev. *Syroboiarsky 27:* Alexandra wrote: "an order from Moscow: the whole suite to be moved from the Kornilov house to the Governor's House . . . no one to be allowed in" (*Skorbnaia pamiatka*, 69).

TOBOLSK 31 MARCH/13 APRIL

1° 6° SATURDAY

Baby slept badly fr. pain & was 4 times sick.

Spent the whole day with Baby

very strong pain—sick

only slept 3 times, 20 minutes.

A little better for 2 hours in the evening & then worse again.

8:30. All-night Vigil.

Tatishchev Valia & Mr. Gibbs have come over to live.

90. ч̄.

Baby slept badly fr. pain & was 4 times sick: Aleksei suffered the worst attack of hemophilia since his sickness in Spala, Poland, in 1912, when many doctors had considered his case hopeless. His recovery was considered nothing less than a miracle, which Alexandra ascribed to Rasputin.

TOBOLSK 1/14 APRIL

Mary of Egypt

SUNDAY

Strong wind grey weather.

Baby slept with intervals of pain.

Sat whole day with him, every half-hour very strong cramp-like pains for 3 m. towards the evening better.

I lunched & dined again next door in Nicholas & Baby's dressing room—18 in the sun.

4:30. tea in Nicholas's room.

6:00–8:00. rested.

sat with the rest.—

Fr. tomorrow on our men may no more go out of the house—

Fr. tomorrow on our men may no more go out of the house: Nicholas's diary: "The detachment committee today resolved that in order to comply with that paper from Moscow [see note for 30 March (12 April)] people living in our house may also no longer go outside, i.e., into town."

TOBOLSK 2/15 APRIL

5th Week of Great Lent

MONDAY

Baby did not sleep the whole night, but no strong pains, Zhilik sat up with him.

Pains less strong to-day, sat whole time with him. Lunched near his bed. Zhilik read much aloud. Went to sleep at 7–11, awake ½ hour & again to sleep.—Rested before dinner

Sat in the evening with the rest.

2 *(15) April:* Nicholas's diary: "In the morning the commandant, together with a commission composed of officers and two riflemen, inspected a number of rooms in our house. The result of this 'search' was the confiscation of sabres from Valia and Mr. Gilliard and a Cossack dagger from me! Again, Kobylinsky explained this measure simply as necessary to calm the riflemen!"

TOBOLSK 3/16 APRIL

TUESDAY

Half snowing half raining. Baby slept very well. Sat with him all day. 37.8°. at 5:30 38.2°.

Mr. Gibbs & Mr. Gilliard read to him.—Dr. contented.

Spent the evening with the others. Rested before dinner.

Baby got late to sleep.

Aunt Olga.

TOBOLSK 4/17 APRIL

WEDNESDAY

Wrote.

Snowing again a little. Baby slept well til 5 & then with interruptions. Spent the day with Baby. 38.5°. feels as yesterday, pains still continue tho' not so strong, Zhilik read much to him. eat a wee bit of fish & a little kissel. I rested fr. 7–8.

10:30–11:00. Nicholas read to us, we worked as usual.— *The Great in the Small.*

V. P. Shneider.

The Great in the Small: By Sergei Nilus; see note for 26 March (8 April). *V. P. Shneider:* Varvara Petrovna Shneider, director of Alexandra's School of Popular Art.

TOBOLSK 5/18 APRIL

THURSDAY

Baby had a hard night. 37.7°

9:20–10:00. Anastasia: Isaiah 34–38.

Spent the day with Baby.

He had more apetite. 37.9°.

4:30. tea as always in Nicholas's room;

rested.

Baby had stronger pains & restless,—but went to sleep towards 11.

Nicholas read aloud.

TOBOLSK 6/19 APRIL

FRIDAY

Bright sunshine & calm:

Baby again slept little—37.7°.

Far stronger pains today, only slept 20 m. in the day, no apetite, such suffering.

12° in the shade

Spent all day with him.

at 5. t:39°. Dr. contented, resorption going well, therefore more pain.

He got to sleep at 10.

2° Nicholas read to us.

Anna Vyrubova 14

Anna Vyrubova 14: Alexandra wrote to Vyrubova about Aleksei's condition: "Yesterday he finally began to eat a little. He is very thin, and the first days reminded me of Spala, you remember. The Lord is merciful. Vladimir Nikolaevich [Derevenko] is contented, he can move around a little, his back hurts and he is tired of lying on it, his bones hurt. I sit with him all day long, and usually I hold his leg, so I have become like his shadow. Of course, we shall have to celebrate *Pascha* [Easter] at home: it will be easier for him, that we are together" (*Russkaia Letopis'*, 4:233).

TOBOLSK 7/20 APRIL

SATURDAY

Grey morning, later sunshine.

Baby 37.9°. had at last a better night. Spent the day with him. 38.2° at 6. pains began to worry him again.

9:00. All-night Vigil. Baby went to sleep.—Snow lying −2°.

Mme. Zizi Naryshkina, Nini Voeikova, Emma Frederiks, Yelizbet, *Cos.* S. θ N.

TOBOLSK 8/21 APRIL

our engagement day (24 years)

SUNDAY

Lovely sunny day, Baby had a midling good night 37.4°.—

11:00. *Obednitsa,* spent the day near his bed, except tea as usual in Nicholas's room & rest before dinner. Nicholas has been obliged to take off his epaulettes, but will wear them still in the house.—Baby 38.1°. pains off & on.

Nicholas read to us in the evenig.

Nicholas has been obliged to take off his epaulettes: The soldiers' committee had moved to abolish the wearing of epaulettes in the special detachment in early January (see entry for 3 [16] January). Kobylinsky testified in 1919 that he told Nicholas at the time: "'Your Majesty, power is slipping out of my hands. They've taken away our epaulettes. I can no longer be of any use to you. With your permission, I would like to leave. My nerves are completely shot. I can't take any more.' His Majesty put one arm around my back. Tears welled up in his eyes, and he told me: 'Yevgeny Stepanovich, on my own behalf, and on behalf of my wife and children, I beg you to stay. You see how we're all forced to endure this. You, too, will have to endure.' Then he embraced me and we exchanged kisses. I remained and decided to endure" (Ross, 298).

TOBOLSK 9/22 APRIL

6th week of Great Lent

MONDAY MORRY'S B.D.

Blowing hard & beginning to snow.

Baby slept with interruptions & pain.

36.6°. Burned letters, arranged papers.

Sat with Baby as usual. After lunch he slept til 4, terribly pale & thin. He played later even cards. More soldiers on foot & on horseback daily almost arrive fr. all over the place.—

37.4°. Nicholas read to us in the evening.

99. ч҃ѳ.

9 (22) April: Gilliard's diary: "The commissary from Moscow arrived to-day with a small detachment; his name is Yakovlef. He has shown his papers to the commandant and soldiers' committee. In the evening he took tea with Their Majesties. Everyone is restless and distraught. The commissary's arrival is felt to be an evil portent, vague but real" (Gilliard, 259). *Burned letters, arranged papers:* Nicholas's diary: "We learned that the extraordinary commissar Yakovlev had arrived from Moscow. . . . The children imagined that he would come today to perform a search, and burned all their letters, and Marie and Anastasia even burned their diaries."

TOBOLSK 10/23 APRIL

TUESDAY

Baby had a bad night because of strong pains. 36.6°.

Snowing again. In the morning the new commissar Yakovlev came to see us (impression of an inteligent highly nervous workman,

10:30. engeneer etc.) Spent the day with Baby. Gay, played cards, read to him. Slept fr. 5–7:15.—37.4°.

Nicholas read to us in the evenig.

100. P̄.

In the morning the new commissar Yakovlev came: Nicholas's diary: "We expected him at 11 o'clock, so Alix was not yet ready. He came in, well-shaved, smiling and embarrassed, and asked whether I were pleased with the guard and the accommodations. Then he went into Aleksei's room almost at a run, without stopping, inspected the remaining rooms and, apologizing for the disturbance, went downstairs. He stepped in to check the others' rooms on the remaining floors in the same rush. A half hour later he appeared again to introduce himself to Alix, again rushed in to see Aleksei and went downstairs. For the time being this was the extent of the inspection of the house."

TOBOLSK 11/24 APRIL

WEDNESDAY

36.6°. Baby had again a restless night with stronger pains

Painted in bed & Tatiana read to me *Spir. Readings*.

Spent the day with Baby working, playing cards.

Olga lunched & dined with us. Aleksei 36.6°. Lovely, sunny day. Rested from 7–8.

Nicholas read to us in the evening.

TOBOLSK 12/25 APRIL

THURSDAY

Baby had a better night 36°.

9:10–10:00. Anastasia: Isaiah 38–42.

Sat with Baby. played cards & worked.

12:15–1:00. Maria: J. Sirach 18–26.

After luncheon the Com. Yakovlev came as I wanted to arrange about the walk to Church for Passion week. Instead of that he anounced by the order of his government (Bolsheviks) that he has to take us all away (to where?) Seeing Baby is too ill wished to take Nicholas alone (if not willing then obliged to use force) I had to decide to stay with ill Baby or accompany him. Settled to accompany him as can be of more need & too risky not knowing where & for what. (we imagine Moscow) Horrible suffering. Marie comes with us, Olga will look after Baby, Tatiana the household & Anastasia will cheer all up. Take Valia, Niuta, Yevgeny Sergeevich offered to go. Chemodurov & Sednyov.

10:30. Took meals with Baby, put few things together, quite small luggage. Took leave of all our people. after evening tea with all. Sat all night with the Children. Baby slept & at 3 went to him til we left. Started at 4:30 in the morning. Horrid to leave precious children. 3 of our rifles went with us.

not knowing where & for what (we imagine Moscow): Kobylinsky testified in 1919: "I then informed His Majesty that Yakovlev apparently wanted to take him to Moscow. Then His Majesty said: 'They want to do that to get me to sign the Treaty of Brest. But I would sooner have my hand cut off than do that.' Extremely agitated, Her Majesty said, 'I'm going, too. Without me there they'll force him to *do* something again—that's exactly what they've done already,' adding something about Rodzianko. Her Majesty was undoubtedly alluding to His Majesty's abdication of the throne" (Ross, 302–303). *Horrible suffering:* Gilliard writes that Alexandra told him: "But the boy is still so ill. . . . Suppose some complication sets in. . . . Oh, God, what ghastly torture! . . . For the first time in my life I don't know what I ought to do" (Gilliard, 260–261). *3 of our rifles went with us:* Three soldiers from the special guard detachment whose loyalty the imperial family could count on.

JOURNEY BY CARRIAGE 13/26 APRIL

FRIDAY

Marie & I in a tarantass.

Nicholas with Com. Yakovlev

Cold, grey & window, crossed the Irtysh.—

After changing horses at 8 & at 12 stopped in a village & took tea with our cold provisions. Road perfectly atrocious, frozen ground wind, snow, water up to the horses' stomachs, fearfully shaken, pain all over. After 4th change, a linchpin popped out & we had to climb over into another basket. Changed 5th time horses & got over into another basket. The others change carriages every time. At 8 got to the town of Ievlevo where we spent the night in house where was the village shop before. We 3 slept in one room we on our beds, Maria on the floor on her mattress, Niuta in her sitting room where we eat of our provisions & our luggage stood. Valia & Yevgeny Sergeevich in our room, our men in another, all on the floor. Got to bed at 10, dead tired & ached all over.—

One does not tell us where we are going fr. Tiumen—some imagine Moscow, the little one are to follow as soon as river free & Baby well.—By turn each carriage lost a wheel or something else smashed. Luggage always late.—heart aches, enlarged, wrote to the children through our first coachman.

tarantass: Springless carriage. *Nicholas with Com. Yakovlev:* Nicholas's diary: "At four in the morning we said farewell to the dear children and sat down in the tarantasses: I with Yakovlev, Alix with Marie, and Valia with Botkin. From among our people, Niuta Demidova, Chemodurov and Sednyov went with us, as did eight riflemen and a mounted escort (Red Army) of ten people." *Our men:* Nicholas's valet Chemodurov and the grand duchesses' manservant Sednyov.

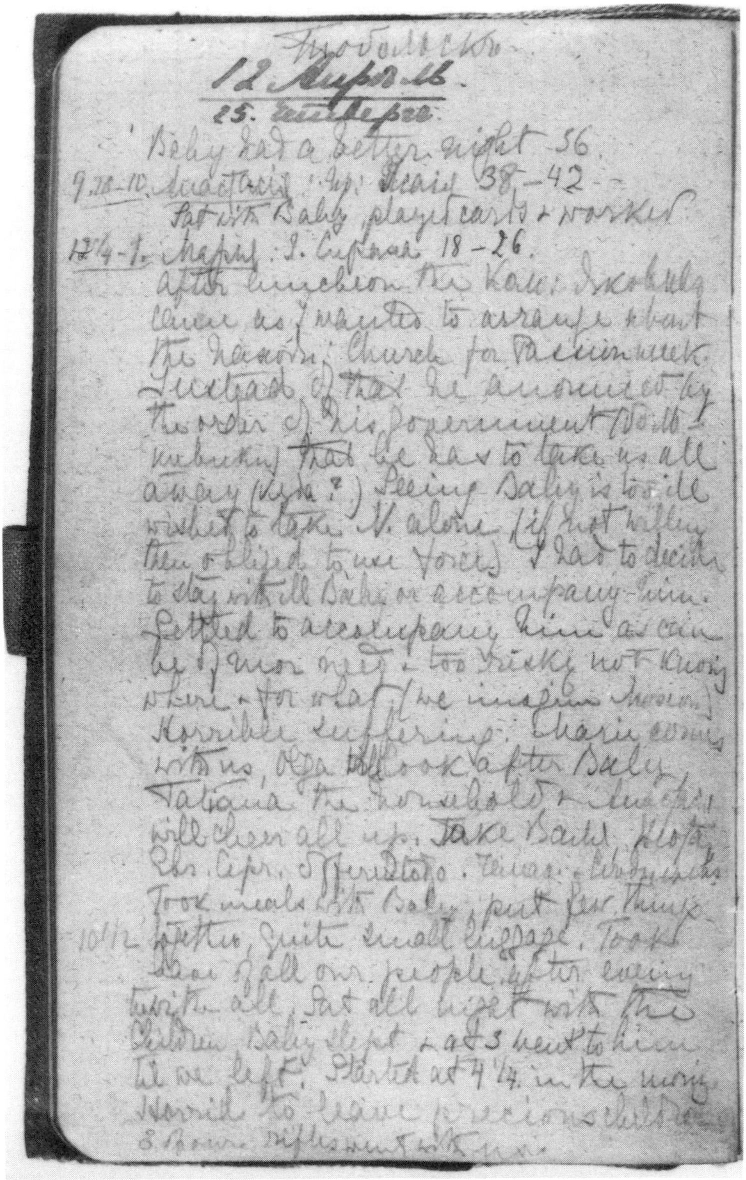

Alexandra's diary entries for 12 (25) and 13 (26) April 1918.

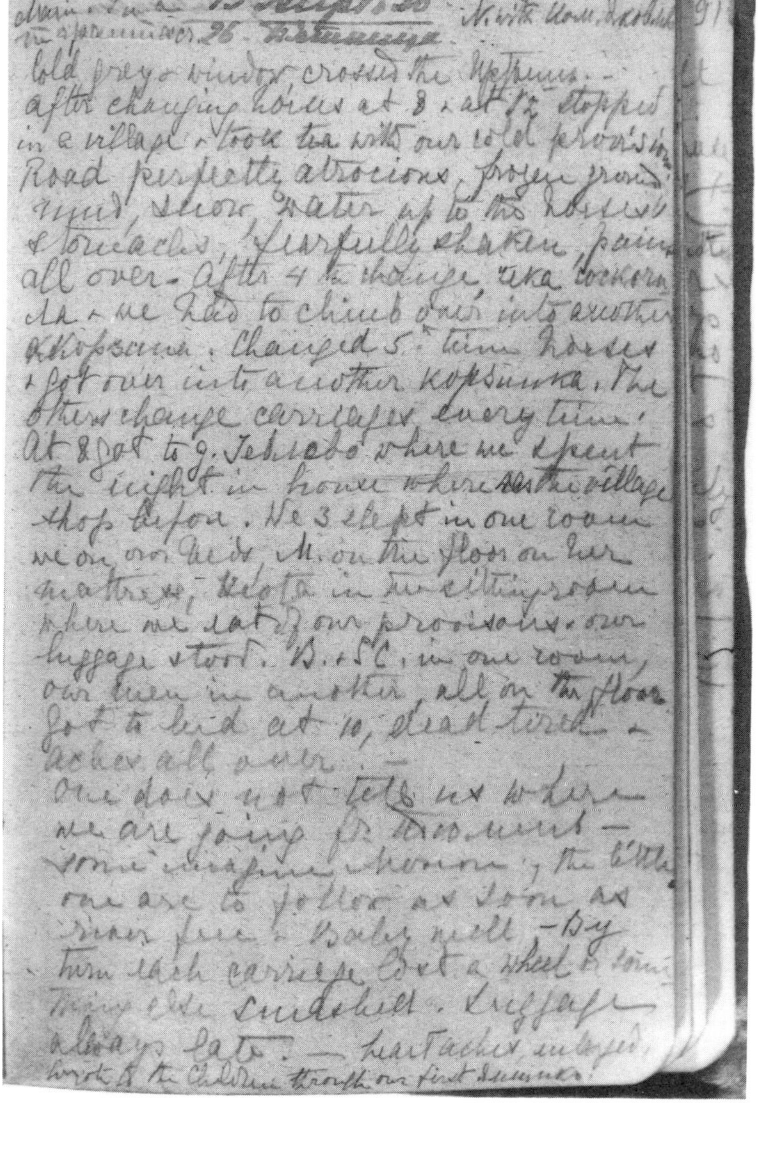
Journey by carriage. 57
[illegible] 13 [illegible] 26 — N. with Mom, [illegible]
[illegible] 26 — [illegible]
Cold grey & windy crossed the [illegible]. —
after changing horses at 8 & at 12 stopped
in a village & took tea with our cold provisions.
Road perfectly atrocious, frozen ground
rigid, snow water up to the horses
stomachs, fearfully shaken, pains
all over. After 4th change, [illegible]
& we had to climb over into another
[illegible]. Changed 5th time horses
& got over into another [illegible]. The
others change carriages every time.
At 8 got to [illegible] where we spent
the night in house where the village
shop before. We 3 slept in one room
we on our beds, M. on the floor on her
mattress, [illegible] in the sitting room
where we eat of our provisions & our
luggage stood. B. & S.C. in one room,
our men in another all on the floor.
Got to bed at 10, dead tired &
aches all over. —
One does not tell us where
we are going for the moment —
some imagine [illegible] the little
ones are to follow as soon as
rivers free & Baby well. — By
turn each carriage lost a wheel or something else smashed. Luggage
always late. — heartaches [illegible]
wrote to the Children through our first [illegible].

JOURNEY BY CARRIAGE 14/27 APRIL

Resurrection of Lazarus

SATURDAY

Got up at 4, had tea, packed up, crossed the river at 5 on foot on planks & then on a ferry. Waited ages before driving off, 7:15. (Com. fidgety, runing about, telegraphing).—Lovely weather, road atrocious. Changes horses, again about 6 times, & our horsemen oftener, as both days the same men. About 12, got to Pokrovskoe changed horses, stood long before our Friend's house, saw his family & friends looking out of the window. At village of Borki took tea & our provisions in a nice peasant's house. Leaving the village, suddenly saw Sedov in the street!—Changed our carriage once. Again all sorts of incidents, but less than yesterday. Stopped in a village school, drank tea with our soldiers. Yevgeny Sergeevich lay down as awful kidney pains. When darkness set in one tied up the bells of our troikas, lovely sunset, & moon. Tore along at a wild rate. Approaching Tiumen a squadron on horseback formed a chain around us & accompanied a far as the station crossed the river on a movable bridge, from 3 versts through the dark town. At midnight got into the train. Wrote 2 to the children in the morning.

Com. fidgety, runing about, telegraphing: At 5:30 A.M. Yakovlev wired Goloshchekin and Didkovsky (see glossary) in Yekaterinburg: "I have received information that your people . . . want to disarm us in order to seize our baggage [i.e., Nicholas II]. Take measures immediately or else there will be bloodshed" (Khrustalëv, 74–80). *stood long before our Friend's house:* Rasputin's house in the village of Pokrovskoe. *suddenly saw Sedov in the street:* Nikolai Yakovlevich Sedov, staff major in Her Imperial Majesty's Crimean Cavalry Regiment, a close friend of Lili Den and Anna Vyrubova. *one tied up the bells of our troikas:* At sunset the bells of the troikas (three-horse teams) were lashed tight to muffle them. *3 versts:* About two miles. *Wrote 2 to the children in the morning:* Alexandra wrote to the children from Ievlevo: "Terribly sad without you. How is Little One sleeping and how does he feel, I hope to God he gets well soon. The journey has been vile: frozen mud, large, deep puddles, ruts—simply unbelievable; what's more, by turn each carriage lost a wheel, and so on, it was nice when this happened to get a rest from the jostling. A change of horses every four hours in the villages" (GARF, f. 673, op. 1, d. 78, l. 3–3ob).

IN THE TRAIN GOING WEST 15/28 APRIL

The Lord's entrance into Jerusalem

SUNDAY. PALM SUNDAY

4:30. Left Tiumen. Scarcely slept.

Glorious sunny weather.

Nicholas & I in 1 compartment, door into Marie's & Niuta's, next door Valia & Yevgeny Sergeevich then our 2 men, then 4 of our rifles. to the other side the 2 Com. & their aids & a dressing room—

Vagai one brought the others soup & a warm dish, otherwise we live on our tea & provisions we brought fr. Tobolsk.

9:00. & dined like that with tea. Sednyov cooked them cutlets. Nazyvaevskaia Station—Marie & Niuta got out once or twice to walk a little.

Wrote to the children—

In the train going west: Alexandra was certain that their train was going west toward Yekaterinburg. *Left Tiumen:* Nicholas's diary: "We all got a good night's rest. We guessed by the names of the stations that we were going in the direction of Omsk. We started to guess: where will they take us after Omsk—to Moscow [west] or Vladivostok [east]? The commissars said nothing, of course." *Vagai:* A station along the way.

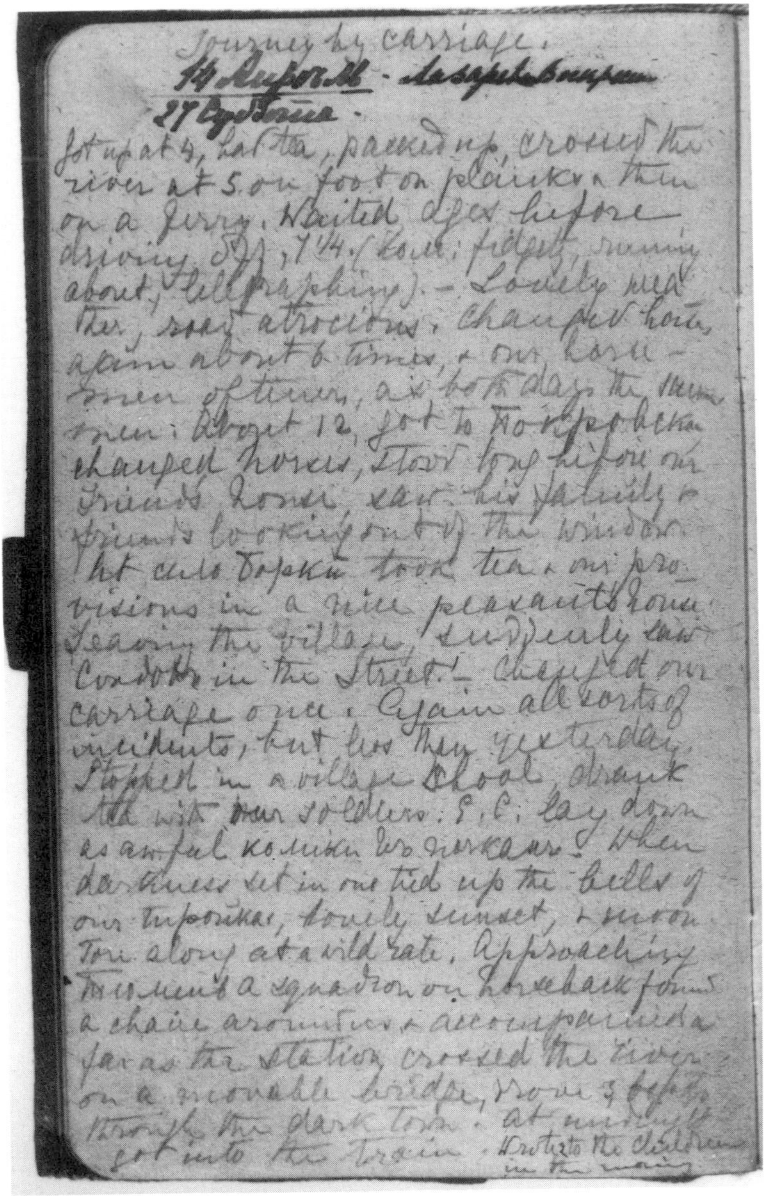

Journey by carriage.
14 Апреля - Воскресенье
27 [illegible]
Got up at 4, had tea, packed up, crossed the river at 5 on foot on planks & then on a ferry. Waited a lot before driving off 7¼. (Kom: fidgety, running about, telegraphing). - Lovely weather, roads atrocious. Changed horses again about 6 times, & our horses oftener, as both days the same ones. About 12, got to Покровская changed horses, stood long before our Friend's house saw his family & friends looking out of the window. At село Борки took tea & our provisions in a nice peasants house. Leaving the village, suddenly saw Cordovs in the street! - Changed our carriage once. Again all sorts of incidents, but less than yesterday. Stopped in a village school, drank tea with our soldiers. E.C. lay down as awful комики [illegible] When darkness set in we tied up the bells of our тройка, lovely sunset, & moon. Tore along at a wild rate. Approaching Тюмень a squadron on horseback formed a chain around us & accompanied us as far as the station crossed the river on a movable bridge, rode [illegible] through the dark town. At midnight got into the train. Wrote to the children in the morning

Alexandra's diary entries for 14 (27) and 15 (28) April 1918.

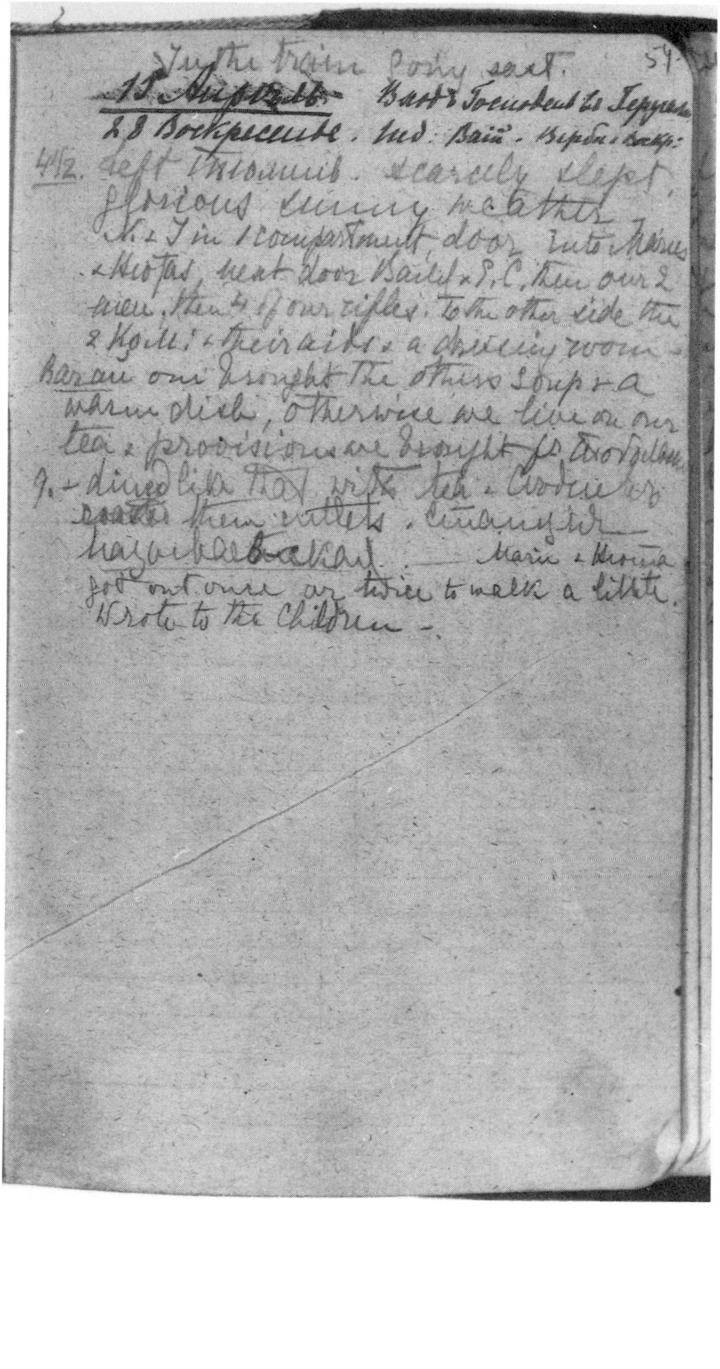
In the train Posly sat. 57
~~15 Апреля~~ Вход Господень во Иерусалим
28 Воскресенье. Нед: Ваий – Вербное воскр:
4½. Left Tobolsk. Scarcely slept. Glorious sunny weather
N. & I in 1 compartment, door into Marie & Nyuta, next door Valia & E.S., then our 2 men, then 4 of our rifles; to the other side the 2 Komis. & their aides & a dressing room –
Kazan one brought the others soup & a warm dish, otherwise we live on our tea & provisions we brought fr. Tobolsk.
9. – dined like that with tea & [illegible] [illegible] them cutlets. [illegible] [illegible] — Marie & Nyuta got out once or twice to walk a little.
Wrote to the Children –

IN THE TRAIN GOING WEST 16/29 APRIL

Passion Week

MONDAY

9:15. siding 52. lovely sunshine. did not reach Omsk & back again,

11:00. again the same station Nazyvaevskaia.

Food was brought for the others. I had
12:10. some coffee.—Masiankaia Station the others got out for a walk.—Soon after they walked again as the axle of one of the carriages got on fire & had to be hooked off.

Sednyov prepared us nice supper again.

Wrote our 5th letter to the children.

Nicholas read to me the Gospels for to-day (the Omsk Sovdep wld. not let us pass Omsk as feared one wished to take us to Japan.) Feel heart much enlarged.

W—

5th letter to the children: Most of Alexandra's letters did not reach her children.

TUESDAY

8:40. Yekaterinburg. Stood ages & moved up & down with the train whilst our two com. Yakovlev & Guzakov spoke with the Sovdep of here. At 3 were told to get out of the train Yakovlev had to give us over to the Ural Region Soviet. Their chief took us three in an open motor, a truck with soldiers armed to their teeth followed us. Drove through bystreets til reached a small house, around wh. high wooden pailings have been placed. Our soldiers not allowed to accompany us. Here a new guard & officer & other civilians, looked through all our baggage. Valia not yet let in. Got our lunch at 4:30. (rations) fr. an hôtel, borshcht & a dish, we 3, Niuta, Yevgeny Sergeevich & our two men eat together. After us the soldiers get the food. We 3 sleep together next room (without door), Niuta in the dining room, then sitting room in wh. sleep Yevgeny Sergeevich & our two men. (Canalisation does not work.)—

15° in the shade Had tea at 9:30. Then one brought beds for the others & found us a basin. Went to bed at 11. Weather was glorious, so warm & sunny. Nicholas read the Bible to us.

Yakovlev had to give us over to the Ural Regional Soviet: Aleksandr Beloborodov (see glossary) wired both Lenin and Sverdlov in Moscow: "Today, 30 April 11 o'clock Petrograd [time] I received from Commissar Yakovlev former tsar Nicholas Romanov, former tsaritsa Alexandra and their daughter Maria Nikolaevna" (GARF, f. 130, op. 2, d. 1109, l. 21). *looked through all our baggage:* The valet Chemodurov testified in August 1918: "One of the men performing the search wrenched the reticule out of Her Majesty's hands, which drew this comment by His Majesty: 'Until now I have been dealing with decent and honest people.' To this Didkovsky replied sharply: 'Do not forget that you are under investigation and arrest'" (Ross, 61–62). *Valia not yet let in:* Valia (Prince Dolgorukov) was falsely accused by the Cheka of harboring weapons and plotting an escape for Nicholas, for which he was arrested and executed.

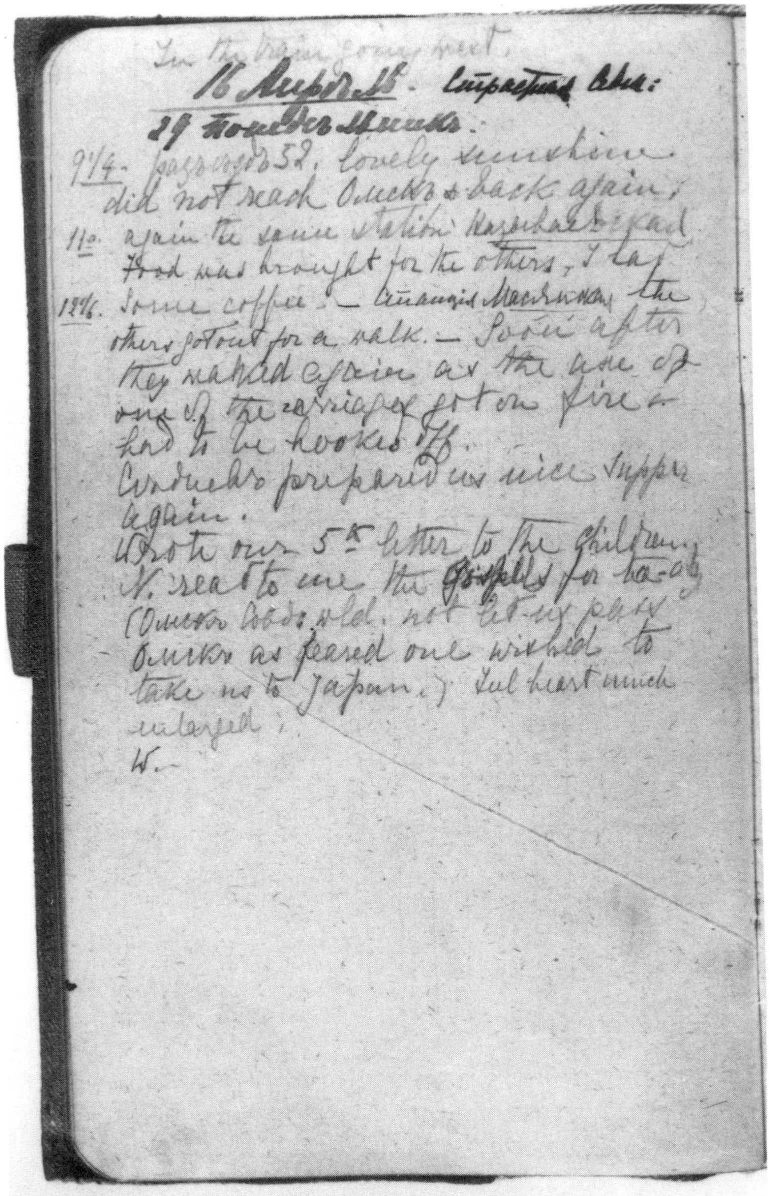

Alexandra's diary entries for 16 (29) and 17 (30) April 1918.

In train — Екатеринбургъ. 55

17 Апрель
30 Вторникъ

8.40. Екатеринбургъ. Stood ages & moved up & down with the train whilst our 2 kom. Яковлевъ & Гузаковъ spoke with the Sov. of here. At 3 were told to get out of the train. Яковлевъ had to give us over to the Ур. Облостн. Совета. Their chief took us 3 in an open motor, a грузовикъ with soldiers armed to their teeth followed us. Drove through bystreets til reached a small house, around wh. high wooden pailings have been placed. Our soldiers not allowed to accompany us. Here a new guard & officer & other civilians, looked through all our baggage. Would not let it in. Got our lunch at 4½ ([illegible]) fr. an hotel, борщъ & a dish, we 3, Nюta, E.C. & our 2 men eat together. After us the soldiers get the food. We 3 sleep together, next room (without door) Nюta, then the dining room, then sitting room in wh. sleep E.C. & our 2 men. (Canalisation does not work.) — Had tea at 9½. Then one brought beds for the others & found us a basin. Went to bed at 11. Weather was glorious, so warm & sunny. I read the Bible to us

YEKATERINBURG 18 APRIL/1 MAY

Ipatiev house

WEDNESDAY

Sunny morning again.

25° in the sun. Remained in bed because of enlarged heart, tired & head ache.

1:15. The others got soup & eggs brought.

I had some good bread

Marie read to me *Spir. Readings.*

3:30. tea, bread & Maltz extract.

Marie read to me, Nicholas sat as his writing table also in our bedroom

reading & writing

8:45. tea. Wrote to the children.

Our Commandant is Avdeev (acc. us fr. Tobolsk it seems) his aid Ukraintsev (former soldier was a beater when Misha went shooting near Borzhom.) (as a little boy Olga played with him at Gagri 15 years ago),—he works in a fabric, receives 300 a month, has a large family.

♡ 3

Ipatiev house. The House of Special Purpose, or the Ipatiev house, was owned by the merchant Nikolai Nikolaevich Ipatiev. *Wrote to the children:* Maria wrote Olga a letter that day, with notes from their parents; it was meant to arrive by Pascha (Easter), four days later: " . . . Christ is risen! I kiss you warmly and bless + you my beloved dear. /Your old mother is always with you in her thoughts, my dear Olga. The three of us are always talking about you and what all of you are up to. The beginning of the trip was unpleasant and depressing; it was better after we got into the train. We don't know how things are going to go here.[Alexandra]/ The Lord protect you. I embrace you thrice, my dear. Papa./ Niuta [Demidova] darns stockings. We make beds together in the morning. Christ be with you. We kiss the nannies and ladies. Your M" (GARF, f. 673, op. 1, d. 78, l. 1–10b). *his aid Ukraintsev:* The imperial family recognized Ukraintsev as one of the beaters from their former hunting parties. He was eventually dismissed from the guard for betraying sympathy toward the Romanovs and sent to the front. *Misha:* Grand Duke Mikhail Aleksandrovich, Nicholas's brother.

Great and Holy Thursday

Beautiful warm sunny, but windy.

Nicholas read the Gospels for the day to us. Soldiers drank up all the water out of the samovar.

10:00. Brought water tea. Heart less enlarged. Wrote postcards. Marie did my hair. Remained on my bed in teagown.—

2:00. Brought luncheon fr. a cafeteria. The others walked for an hour in the tiny garden.—Maria read to me.

6:30. tea.

Nicholas read to me, Job.

Arrayed our Images on a table in the sitting room, for reading later

9:00. supper.

We all 7 sat together & Nicholas & Yevgeny Sergeevich change about read 12 Gosp.—

Wrote to the children.

Soldiers drank up all the water out of the samovar: The Romanovs' treatment under arrest took a sharp turn for the worse. From Avdeev's memoirs: "As soon as they were brought to Yekaterinburg, the family's sham titles were dispensed with, and it was proposed that both servants and the surrounding people address the former tsar and his family by first name and patronymic. This petty formality on our part irked them greatly, particularly Alexandra Fyodorovna, who asked me: 'And why has no one dispensed with addressing one by title before this?' I replied that now they were in the hands of genuine revolutionaries. . . . Next came a second measure: the former tsar, his family and retainers were no longer permitted to live like tsars" (Avdeev, 200). *Arrayed our Images on a table in the sitting room, for reading later:* Alexandra arranged her icons in preparation for reading the gospels aloud, as is done in church, on Great and Holy Thursday of Passion Week.

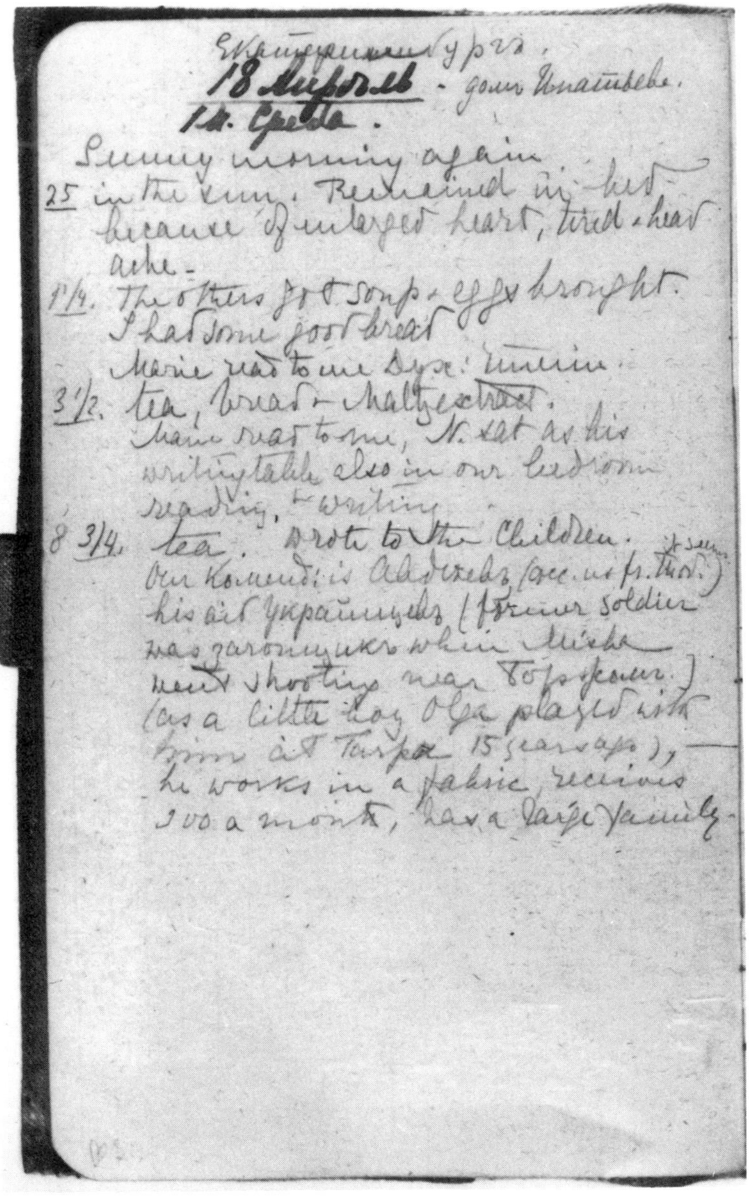

Екатеринбургъ.
18 Апрѣль - домъ Ипатьева.
1 М. Среда.

Sunny morning again
25 in the sun. Remained in bed
because of enlarged heart, tired & head
ache.
1 1/4. The others got soup & eggs brought.
I had some good bread
Marie read to me Духов: Чтение.
3 1/2. tea, bread & maltzextract.
Marie read to me, N. sat at his
writingtable also in our bedroom
reading & writing
8 3/4. tea. Wrote to the Children. It seems
Our Komend: is Авдеевъ (acc. is fr. that)
his aid Украинцевъ (former soldier
was загонщикомъ when Misha
went shooting near Боржомомъ.)
(as a little boy Olga played with
him at Tarpa 15 years ago), —
he works in a fabric, receives
400 a month, has a large family.

Alexandra's diary entries for 18 April (1 May) and 19 April (2 May) 1918.

Екатеринбургъ

19 Апр. 18.

2. Ма. Вел. Четвергъ

Beautiful warm sunny, but windy.
N. read the Gospels for the day to us. Soldiers
drank up all the water out of the самоваръ.
10 Brought water for tea. Heart less enlarged. Wrote
postcards. Marie did my hair. Re-
main on my bed in teagown. —
2. brought luncheon fr a restorant.
The others walked for an hour in
the tiny garden. — M. read to me.
6½. tea.
N. read to me Job.
Arranged our Images on a table in
the sittingroom, for reading later.
9. Supper.
We all sat together. N. & S.C. change
about read 12 Евангелiй; —
Wrote to the children. —

YEKATERINBURG 20 APRIL/3 MAY

3° *Great and Holy Friday*

7° Snowed a little in the night & in the daytime & bright sunshine.

Nicholas read the Gospel & Job to us both.

Dressed at 12:30. I remained on my bed in teagown.

3:20. At last brought luncheon.

6:00. tea. others walked before ½ hour.

Nicholas read to us. *The Great in the Small.* & then the Gospels for the evening.

10:20. brought supper. Sednyov prepared me vermicelli.

Wrote to the children

Syroboiarsky 28, p.c. w. by Niuta

Nicholas read the Gospel & Job: In reading Scripture aloud to the family, Nicholas compensated in part for their inability to participate in church services. *Sednyov prepared me vermicelli.* As Alexandra was ill, Sednyov occasionally cooked something especially for her from the provisions brought from Tobolsk. *Wrote to the children:* This letter has not been discovered. Gilliard testified in 1919 that in this letter Alexandra reported that all of their belongings had been examined, "including medicines" (Alexandra's code word for jewels), and then used "very cautious expressions to indicate that upon leaving Tobolsk they should take all their jewels with them but with the greatest precautions" (Ross, 233).

YEKATERINBURG 21 APRIL/4 MAY

Great and Holy Saturday

1° Slightly snowing. Wrote to the children 8th time. Nicholas read to us Gospel & book

1:40. Brought their luncheon. Nicholas had a bath.

2:00. Sednyov cooked vermicelli again for me.

3:00. Had a bath. Niuta too.

Lay down again. Wrote to the children

the others went out for 20 m.

5:30. tea.

Nicholas read to us. Arrayed our images on table.

8:20. Priest & Deacon came & served matins—soldiers of the guard came too.—

9:00. Dined.

10:00. Went to bed.—Marie read to me.

Wrote to the children 8th time: Alexandra's letter was seized by the Ural Soviet and has never been discovered. Nicholas's diary: "Wrote several lines each in letters to our daughters from Alix and Marie and drew a plan of this house." This plan of the Ipatiev house later figured in many Chekist documents as evidence of an escape plot. Avdeev recalled with pleasure confronting Nicholas with the intercepted drawing: "He tripped over his words like a schoolboy and said he hadn't known it was forbidden to send plans" (Avdeev, 204). *Priest & Deacon came & served matins:* Fr. Anatoly Grigorievich Meledin and Deacon Vasily Afanasievich Buimirov.

YEKATERINBURG 22 APRIL/5 MAY

Pascha

SUNDAY

-3° Marie read to me *Spir. Readings,* & Nicholas the Gospel & French book.

1:00. Sednyov prepared us luncheon warmed up yesterday's food, I was up too & then lay down again. Wrote to the children. The others walked a little. Had coco. Nicholas read *Small in the Great* to us.

5:00. tea—sun came out.

Nicholas read the evening's Gospel to us.

8:00. Supper, I had it with them.

We sat in Yevgeny Sergeevich's room for an hour.

-4° Talked with Ukraintsev.

Early to bed again.

Pascha: Easter. In his diary entry for this date Nicholas drew another plan of the Ipatiev house. Small in the Great: Alexandra meant *The Great in the Small.*

YEKATERINBURG 23 APRIL/6 MAY

Holy Martyr Alexandra, Holy Great Martyr George the Victory-Bearer

MONDAY

-2° Slight snow lying & sunshine.

Nicholas read Gospel to us & *Great in the Small.*

Wrote to the Children—

1:00. Lunched with the others like yesterday

7:00. Sednyov prepared the food.

Lay down again.

3:00. The others went out in the wee garden 40 steps square

coco. Nicholas read to us. Marie painted.

5:00. tea. Maria read to me *Spir. Readings*.

-5° *8:00.* Supper like luncheon only I remained lying; later we sat in Botkin's room.

Holy Martyr Alexandra: The Church commemorates Empress Alexandra, wife of Diocletian, on this date, which was Alexandra's name day.

YEKATERINBURG 24 APRIL/7 MAY

Bright Week

2° TUESDAY

Sunshine & clouds change about,

Wrote to the Children.

Nicholas read the Gospel to us & *Great in the Small.*

Sednyov prepared me vermicelli, so had my lunch at 1:45, the others had theirs only brought at 2.

Nicholas read to us.

3:00–4:00. The others walked. coco.

Nicholas read to us Maeterlinck.

5:15. tea.

Nicholas read to us & we played chicane.

8:15. Supped with the others, then played bezique with Nicholas, & Maria & Yevgeny Sergeevich also played cards.

Bright Week: Easter Week. *Nicholas read to us Maeterlinck:* Nicholas alternated readings from the Bible with Turgenev's *Spring Torrents*, J. K. Green's *Short History of the English People*, the novels of Vsevolod Solovyov, and Maurice Maeterlinck's *La Sagesse et la Destinée* (Wisdom and destiny) (*Dnevniki*, 670–676).

5° WEDNESDAY

Sunshine & strong wind.

Nicholas as daily read the Gospel to us & then *Great in the Small.*

1:15. Had Sednyov: excellent vermic. & bread & butter

1:30. Lunch was brought to the others.

Snowed a little. Wrote to the children.

Lay with shut eyes as head continued to ache.

4:00–5:00. The others walked in the sunshine.

Marie read to me after tea.

8:15. Supped—got first wire fr. children

Played bezique.

Cannot get them to tell us anything about Valia.

got first wire fr. children: Olga wired the maid Anna Demidova from Tobolsk on the previous day: "Thanks letters. All well. Little One already been garden. We are writing. Olga" (GARF, f. 673, op. 1, d. 74, l. 1).

YEKATERINBURG 26 APRIL/9 MAY

−1° THURSDAY.

Wrote 14th time to children.

Sun & clouds. Continue sleeping badly & having a headache.

Nicholas read the Gospel to us & lesson for the day

Every morning have to get out of bed for the guards, head of the guards & Com. who come to see if we are there.

1:00. Sednyov: prepared my vermicelli.

2:10. At last brought the others their food.

Marie & Niuta washed my hair.

Slightly snowing; & then sun appeared.

4:30. The others went out.

5:15. tea. Marie read to me *Spir. Readings:*

Nicholas read to us.

8:00. Supper wh. I took with the others.

Then played cards in Yevgeny Sergeevich's room—

come to see if we are there: Avdeev wrote in his memoirs: "The prisoners' daily schedule was as follows: they rose at nine in the morning and had tea at ten, after which there was a check, which consisted of the commandant's inspecting the rooms, verifying that the prisoners were present " (Avdeev, 203).

2° FRIDAY

8:15. Told us to get up as Com. wished to see us before changing in ¼ of an hour & to look at the rooms.

0° Yesterday they changed 3 times—

Greyish weather.—snowing slightly

Wrote 15th time to the Children—

Maria read to me *Spir. Readings.*

6° Nicholas read to us.

1:45. Lunch was brought.

3:00. The others went out.

4:15. Had tea with them.

Again people came to ask now how much money we all have (we both have) & all had to write down the sum & give it up to the Sovdep to take care of.

Nicholas read to us Leikin.

8:15. Dined with the others.

Played cards in Yevgeny Sergeevich's room.

talked with the Chief of the Guards.—

Com. wished to see us: Nicholas's diary: "At 8:15 we were supposed to get up and get dressed in order to receive yesterday's deputy commandant, who had handed us over to a new one—with a kind face reminiscent of an artist's." *Wrote 15th time to the Children:* Alexandra and (mainly) Maria wrote to Tobolsk that day: "We miss the quiet and calm life in Tobolsk. We get nasty surprises here almost daily. Members of the regional [executive] committee were just here and asked each one of us how much money we were carrying. We had to sign for it. Since Papa and Mama haven't a single kopeck with them, they signed that they had nothing, and I signed for the 16 rubles and 17 kopecks that Anastasia gave me for the trip. They took all the money everyone else had for safekeeping by the committee; leaving everyone just a little and issuing them receipts. They warned us that there was no guarantee we wouldn't be searched again. Who would think that after fourteen months of imprisonment we would be treated like this? We hope you have it better—like when we were there" (GARF, f. 685, op. 1, d. 276, l. 1–20b).

YEKATERINBURG 28 APRIL/11 MAY

2° SATURDAY

Bright sunshine. Slept better.

Nicholas read the Gospel & lesson to us.

Wrote 16th time to the children.

11:30–12:00. The others walked. Got a wire fr. Olga.

9° Nicholas read to us. Lunched with the others.

3:00. They went out.

Nicholas read to us.

Took tea together.

Nicholas read to us.

9:30. Supper was brought.

Played cards.

Got a wire fr. Olga: Olga's message: "All thank you [for] Pascha postcards. Little One slowly improving, feeling well. Kiss you warmly. Olga" (GARF, f. 685, op. 1, d. 286, l. 1).

YEKATERINBURG 29 APRIL/12 MAY

Anniv. of Otsou

4° SUNDAY

Sunny & windy & clouds

Wrote postcard to the children No. 17

10:15. Only got our tea. Head continues again & slept very little.

15° Nicholas read to us.

1:45. Brought luncheon—with the others

3:00–4:00. Sat in the garden—

Nicholas read to us—

5:30. tea with the others

Maria read to us *Spir. Readings.*

Nicholas finished reading *Great in the Small.*

8:00. Supper—

Played cards.

frost. Had a bath.

Anniv. of Otsou: In 1891 in the small Japanese town of Otsu, Nicholas, still the heir to the throne, was nearly assassinated by an enraged local policeman who struck him over the right ear with a saber (Radzinsky, 28–29).

YEKATERINBURG 30 APRIL/13 MAY

2d Week of Pascha

5° MONDAY (WEEK OF ST. THOMAS THE APOSTLE)

Glorious sunshine.

Wrote 18th time to the children—p.c.

10° 10:30 the others went out walking.

19° Nicholas read to us, cards with Maria

1:00. Sednyov gave me my lunch.

3:30. One only brought the others their food.

Sat out for 1 h. & 20 m.

5:30. tea.

9° Nicholas read to us & we as usual played cards.

8:30. Supped. Played cards.

Mme. Syroboiarskaia 32. p.c. thr. Niuta.

YEKATERINBURG 1/14 MAY

10° TUESDAY

Beautiful warm morning.

20° Wrote 19th time to the children p.c—

10:30 the others walked for 40 m.

1:00. Lunched.

3:00. Only let us now be out ½ an hour twice daily.

Nicholas read to us, played cards with Maria

5:00. Tea. Nicholas read again.

8:00. Supper—

cards—

The guard changed after a week.

Only let us now be out ½ an hour twice daily: Nicholas's diary: "By noon, there was a change in the guard using the same special crew of front-line soldiers—Russians and Latvians. The chief of the guards is a young, imposing person. Today we were told, via Botkin, that we are allowed only one hour a day to walk; when we asked why, the acting commandant answered: 'To make it like a prison regime.'"

YEKATERINBURG 2/15 MAY

10° WEDNESDAY

17° Wrote 20th time to the children.

Nicholas read as usual the Gospel, Acts to us 2.

Splendid weather, a nice breeze.

They were told not to go out this morning. An old man painted all the windows white fr. outside, so only at the top can see a bit of sky & it looks as tho' there were a thick fogg, not at all cosy.

1:30. Lunched. Sednyov feels unwell & lies.

Nicholas read to us.

3:15. Were let into the garden for an hour.

Nicholas read again & we played patiences.

5:00. tea.

8:00. Supper.

cards.

Sednyov infl: 38.6°.

us 2: Probably Alexandra and Maria. *told not to go out this morning:* Nicholas's diary: "Establishment of the 'prison regime' continued and was evident when an old housepainter came and whitewashed every window in every room. Now it's like a fog looking in at every window. Went for a walk at 3:15 and at 4:10 they herded us home. There wasn't a single off-duty soldier in the garden. The chief of the guards didn't talk with us because the whole time there was one commissar or another in the garden watching us, him, and the sentries! The weather was very good, but in the rooms it had become dim. Only the dining room was improved, because they took down the rug covering the windows!"

YEKATERINBURG 3/16 MAY

THURSDAY

They smeared over the therm: so can't see temp; seems fine weather,

Nicholas read to us. Head continues aching.

1:30. Luncheon—

3:00–4:00. Let in the garden—

5:00. tea—

Wrote 21st time to the children.

8:30. Supper, 3 candles in glasses

cards—by light of one candle.

Sednyov half up.

Received coffee & chocolate fr. Ella. She has been sent out from Moscow & is at Perm (we read in the papers.)

Supper, 3 candles in glasses: A problem with the electrical wiring in the Ipatiev house took several days to repair; meanwhile, the family used candles. *She has been sent out from Moscow:* Grand Duchess Yelizaveta Fyodorovna (see glossary) was arrested by the Cheka and exiled first to Perm, then to Yekaterinburg, where she was denied permission to see her sister Alexandra.

YEKATERINBURG 4/17 MAY

FRIDAY

Great treat, cup of coffee.

Raining a little—have a fire burning, is so damp.

3 weeks today we left Tobolsk.

Maria Wrote 22 time to the children—& to Ella, & Zinochka Tolstaia (did not send it.)

1:50 Luncheon.

Half an hour out in slight rain.

Heard the children are already traveling.

5:00. tea.

Nicholas read to us.

8:00. Supper by candle light again.

cards.

& to Ella: Maria wrote to her aunt Yelizaveta Fyodorovna thanking her for the package she had sent. *Heard the children are already traveling:* Nicholas's diary: "Learned that the children had left Tobolsk, but Avdeev did not say when. In the afternoon he himself opened the door of the locked room we had set aside for Aleksei. It appeared large and lighter than we had supposed, as it has two windows; our stove heats it well. We walked for half an hour because of rain." *Supper by candle light again:* Nicholas's diary: "The commandant, his assistant, the chief of the guards and the electricians were running through all the rooms fixing the wiring, but we dined in darkness nonetheless."

YEKATERINBURG 5/18 MAY

SATURDAY

Been raining again.

Maria read to me *Spir. Readings*. Nicholas read to us.

1:00. Had my lunch, the others

2:00. had theirs only brought at 2.

3:30–4:00. In the garden, grey, cold—

5:00. tea.

8:00. I had my supper, the others

9:00. only at 9.

cards.

Had a bath.

YEKATERINBURG 6/19 MAY

Righteous Job the Long-Suffering

SUNDAY. NICHOLAS'S 50TH B.D.

Glorious, bright sunshine.

11:30. Easter service of intercession.

The others went out.

1:30. Luncheon—

3:00–4:30. sat in the garden, divine weather

5:15. tea.

Nicholas read to us.

8:30. supper.

Cannot find out whether the children left or not—
get no letters from anybody.—

cards.

Righteous Job the Long-Suffering . . . Nicholas's 50th B.D.: Nicholas was born on the Day of Job. *Nicholas read to us: The Blue and Gold* by Arkady Averchenko, a popular Russian humorist, playwright, and editor.

YEKATERINBURG 7/20 MAY

3d Week of Pascha (the Holy Myrrh-Bearing Women)

MONDAY

Sunshine & clouds.

1:00. For the first time lunch was brought punctually.

The Guard and Chief of the Guard changed after a week.—

2:30. Sat out over an hour.

5:00. tea.

Nicholas read to us, then he had a bath.

Maria *Spiritual Readings.*

9:00. The others had their supper.

Played cards, nearly all times by candle light as electricity in my room wld. not burn. The Kom: scratched off the paint covering the thermom: so now can see again the degrees. A week no news fr. the children

Nicholas read to us: Nicholas continued reading Averchenko's *Blue and Gold.*

7° TUESDAY

Been pouring.

Maria *Spir. Readings*. Nicholas read as usual the Gospel & lesson of the day.

3 weeks here to-day.

Lunched late.

Heard children come probably to-morrow or Thursday

Have given us a room for Baby, 1 for the gentlemen

11° & 1 for the men (where the guard was at first).—

3:30. Nicholas & Maria went out.—

5:00. tea.

sunshine after slight thunder at 3.

Maria took a bath.

8:45. Only had their supper.

cards.

Have given us a room for Baby: Nicholas's diary: "Avdeev offered to let us inspect two rooms next to the dining room; the guard is now housed in the basement."

YEKATERINBURG 9/22 MAY

Translation of the Relics of St. Nicholas the Wonder-Worker

9° WEDNESDAY K. P.'S NAME DAY

Dressed by 11.

at 1:45. Brought the others their luncheon

Fine weather—

Sat out for an hour—

5:00. tea.

Nicholas read to us. No news of the children—

8:00. Supper—

cards.

YEKATERINBURG 10/23 MAY

1° THURSDAY

All covered in snow. 4 weeks we left Tobolsk.—

Towards 11 the girls suddenly turned up with Aleksei—thank God—such joy to have them again.

Nobody else let in all day except for the cook Kharitonov & boy Sednyov,—

only hand luggage brought—no news about the rest.

Luncheon, tea, supper as usual.

Went out for 1/4 of an hour, snow & dirt lying,—

Put Baby into Marie's bed, & arranged the 4 girls on cloaks & cushions on the floor in the adjoining room.

Kharitonov on short sopha, Sednyov on two chairs.—after night Baby woke up every hour from pain in his knee, slipped & hurt it when getting into bed.*—Cannot walk yet, one carries him. Lost 14 pounds since his illness.—

Saw fr. far in the night great fire burning.—

*Tore sinews in the knee most probably.—

Towards 11 the girls suddenly turned up with Aleksei: Nicholas's diary: "During the course of an hour in the morning we were told that the children were a few hours from town, next, that they had arrived at the station, and finally, that they had arrived at the house, although their train had been here since two in the morning! What an enormous joy it was to see them again and to embrace them after the four-week separation and the uncertainty. There was no end to the mutual questions and answers. The poor things had suffered a lot of moral anguish both in Tobolsk and during the three-day trip." Gilliard, who accompanied the children, wrote: "We reached Ekaterinburg in the night, the train being stopped at some distance from the station. . . . The next morning . . . Nagorny, the sailor attached to Alexis Nicolaevitch, passed my window, carrying the sick boy in his arms; behind him came the Grand-Duchesses, loaded with valises and small personal belongings. I tried to get out, but was roughly pushed back into the carriage by the sentry. . . . Tatiana Nicolaievna came last, carrying her little dog and struggling to drag a heavy brown valise. It was raining, and I saw her feet sink into the mud at every step. Nagorny tried to come to her assistance; he was roughly pushed back by one of the commissaries" (Gilliard, 269).

YEKATERINBURG 11/24 MAY

Ludwig's B.D. May's B.D.

FRIDAY

Baby & I had our meals in our bedroom: his pains varied.

Lunched at 2—

Vladimir Nikolaevich came to see Baby & change his compressings but in Avdeev's presence so he cld. not say a word.—

Chemodurov left as not feeling well—Was completely undressed & searched before leaving the house.—After supper Nagorny & Trup (& Joy) came—2 hours questioned & searched. All our other people are being sent back to Tobolsk, only won't know where Trina, Nastinka, Tatishchev, & Volkov have been taken & Yevgeny Sergeevich wrote petition for Avdeev to take to the Regional Committee to beg for Zhilik, as absolutely indispensable, he shld. be with Baby, who suffers very much.—

Baby slept in his room with Nagorny—the four girls next door, not all beds brought yet.

Baby had bad night again.

Ludwig's B.D. May's B.D.: Birthday of Alexandra's brother-in-law Prince Ludwig (Louis) of Battenberg and the Countess Maria Illarionovna Musina-Pushkina, a former nurse in military hospitals. *Vladimir Nikolaevich came:* Doctor Vladimir Nikolaevich Derevenko was permitted to visit the Ipatiev house to treat the tsarevich, but only under the supervision of Chekists. *Chemodurov left:* Nicholas's diary: "Decided to let my old Chemodurov have a rest and took on Trupp for a while in his place. Only in the evening were he and Nagorny allowed in, and then they were interrogated and searched for an hour and a half in the commandant's room." *After supper Nagorny & Trup:* Before the Chekists admitted Nagorny and the footman Trupp (see glossary) to the Ipatiev house, both servants had to sign statements that they were voluntarily submitting to the confinement regime and sharing the fate of the imperial family. *Joy:* Aleksei's pet spaniel. *Trina, Nastinka, Tatishchev, & Volkov:* The first three were imprisoned and later executed; Alexandra's valet Volkov managed to flee. *Yevgeny Sergeevich wrote petition:* The petition to Beloborodov, which sought the admission of Sidney Gibbs as well as Gilliard, was not granted.

YEKATERINBURG 12/25 MAY

Aunt Helena's B.D.

3° SATURDAY

Baby spent the day like yesterday, swelling wee bit less but pains off & on very strong. Only drank a cup of tea & a plate of sowermilk. Vladimir Nikolaevich came with Avdeev & Com.—4 people of the comittee looked in later. They look through the childrens' things, only necessary trunks are brought up. They walked a little.

Snowing hard. Don't wish to let Zhilik in, have asked again.

Baby took a little food & then went to sleep.

played bez. with Nicholas & then early to bed.

Aunt Helena's B.D.: The birthday of Helena, duchess of Schleswig-Holstein, Queen Victoria's daughter and Alexandra's aunt.

YEKATERINBURG 13/26 MAY

4th Sunday of Pascha

2° SUNDAY. (SUNDAY OF THE PARALYTIC)

Everything covered by snow, brighter. Baby had again a bad night but spent a better day. Several times had the blue light, eat a little more. He Lay in our room all day. Lunch was brought again late. Others went out a little. When Vladimir Nikolaevich came there was also a Dr. in the room—The Commissar & Commandant & Chief of the Guards have been looking through all the childrens things again. The swelling is a little less. No news of our people.

there was also a Dr. in the room: This was Yakov Yurovsky, the future commandant of the Ipatiev house, replacing Avdeev, and Nicholas's executioner (see glossary). He was trained as an army medical assistant. Nicholas, too, wrote in his diary that all had taken Yurovsky for a doctor.

YEKATERINBURG 14/27 MAY

Coronation Day

6° MONDAY

20° Bright sunshine. Baby had again not good night, Yevgeny Sergeevich sat up part of the night so as to let Nagorny sleep.

2:00. Lunch brought.

Baby spent the day in our room. Vladimir Nikolaevich did not come, don't know why.

Children darning linnen with Niuta—

At 6:30 Sednyov & Nagorny were taken off to the District Committee. don't know the reason. The others played cards with Baby. On the whole better, tho' at times very strong pains.

Yevgeny Sergeevich spent the night with Baby.

14 (27) May: Nicholas's diary: "In the evening, an examination of the daughters' things continued in their presence. The sentry standing under our window shot into our house because he thought he'd seen someone moving at the window (after ten o'clock at night)—I think he was just fooling around with his rifle, as sentries always do." *Coronation Day:* The twenty-second anniversary of Nicholas's coronation. *Sednyov & Nagorny were taken off to the District Committee:* Former sailors on the imperial yacht *Shtandart*, Sednyov and Nagorny were imprisoned.

YEKATERINBURG 15/28 MAY

9° TUESDAY

Poured in the night. Baby slept on the whole well, tho' woke up every hour—pains less strong.

20° Came to our room again.

They got their lunch only at 2:25.

They went out for an hour—

Vladimir Nikolaevich came at last, can't speak to him as Avdeev always present. I asked when at last Nagorny will be let in again as don't know how we shall get on without him—Avdeev answers does not know—fear that shant see him nor Sednyov again.

Baby suffered very much for a while, then after medic. & candle got better. After tea I cut Nicholas's hair for the first time.—

15° After supper Baby was carried in his bed to his room again. Pains stronger.

We were in bed by 11.

YEKATERINBURG 16/29 MAY

Midfeast of Pentecost

14° WEDNESDAY

Baby's night was better.

Glorious weather.

Tatiana sowed my j.

20° Baby & I lunched in his room & then he came to our room. slept a little before Vladimir Nikolaevich came (& new Commandant.) put him half a plaster of Paris splint.

15° the others walked as usual, & in the morning too.

Baby was carried back to his room to dine, I went to bed after supper with strong headache.

Tatiana sowed my j.: Fearing more searches and confiscations of jewels, the imperial family sewed them into articles of clothing.

YEKATERINBURG 17/30 MAY

14° THURSDAY

Baby had a better night 37.4°, spent the day in our room, very rarely pain in the day (today.)

22° Vladimir Nikolaevich came (Avdeev.) 37.6°. found swelling in the knee 1 cm. less & in the inside also
15° less, therefore probably higher temp fr. resorption. 38.9½°. before dinner pains became stronger, cramps, took him to his room.

Got to sleep at 9.

The others went out in the afternoon.

No news of anybody.

Played a little bezique with Nicholas before going to bed.

YEKATERINBURG 18/31 MAY

10° FRIDAY

Poured in the night.

Baby's night the same 36.9½°

I remained in bed as feeling very giddy & eyes ache so.

1:40 Baby brought over at 1 to us—Luncheon.

Slight rain, others went out.

Hammering hard, making wooden pailing before Baby's windows higher. Vladimir Nikolaevich not let in as Avdeev was not there. The others went out. Remained whole day with shut eyes, head got worse towards the evening. Supper brought at 6 but they only eat it at 8, warmed up. Baby 37.6°.

After supper Baby was carried to his room—had rather cramps in his knee again.—

YEKATERINBURG 19 MAY/1 JUNE

11° SATURDAY

Night better. Early morning, sun.

9° Came over to me before luncheon. I spent the day in bed, feeling week & nasty in the head—.

Baby 37.6°. slept a little in the day.

12° The others went out.

Grey weather—

5:30. Vladimir Nikolaevich & Avdeev came after supper. Baby was carried to his room. His head ached a little, but he went quickly to sleep. The children washed handkerchiefs again—

YEKATERINBURG 20 MAY/2 JUNE

Uncovering of the Relics of St. Alexis

12° SUNDAY 5TH SUNDAY OF PASCHA

(SUNDAY OF THE SAMARITAN WOMAN)

19° Glorious sunny weather. Baby had a pretty good night. Dressed; took Baby into the big room with

11:20 his bed & had *Obednitsa*. A new Priest.

The others went out. 25° in the sun—& 30°. After lunch, i.e. 3:15 they went out again, Baby slept some time—played cards with him.

Vladimir Nikolaevich & Avdeev came.

After supper he was carried back to his room by Nicholas, Trup & Kharitonov—& went soon to sleep.

I played a little bezique with Nicholas & early to bed, as still not feeling very well & weak.—

Obednitsa. *A new Priest:* Protopriest Fr. Ioann Storozhev (see glossary).

YEKATERINBURG 21 MAY/3 JUNE

Holy Equal-to-the-Apostles King Constantine and Helen
Eng. Georgie's B.D.

18° MONDAY

Baby had a good night 36.5°, was brought to our room before 11.

Lunch came only at 2.

25° The others walked in the morning & afternoon on the whole only an hour is aloud.

Very warm wind—

Played patiences, cards—

After dinner he was carried back to his room & very soon went to sleep.

Vladimir Nikolaevich was not let in as Avdeev was not there.

15° I played bezique with Nicholas & went to bed at 10.

Poured hard in the night.

Eng. Georgie's B.D.: The birthday of the English king, George V, cousin of Nicholas and Alexandra. *Baby had a good night:* Nicholas's diary: "Downstairs in the guards' quarters there was another gun shot, and the commandant came to inquire whether the bullet had gone through the floor. Aleksei had no pains whatsoever; as always, he spends the day in bed in our room."

YEKATERINBURG 22 MAY/4 JUNE

16° TUESDAY

Baby slept well, but less so than the night before.

Fine, bright morning.

Baby spent the day in my room—apetite still not good.

The others went out in the afternoon—

Vladimir Nikolaevich & Avdeev came at 7.

Knee much less swollen (3 cm.) he may be carried out tomorrow.—

I had a bath at 10.

Lenin gave the order that the clocks have to put 2 hours ahead (economy of electricity) so at 10 they told us it was 12.

At 10 strong thunderstorm.

The committee has not given the permission for Aleksei whilst he is ill to be out as long as he likes, but we all only an hour as before!!—

Lenin gave the order: As chairman of the Council of People's Commissars, Lenin signed a decree on 30 May calling for "clocks all over Russia to be set two hours ahead for the summer season" as of ten P.M. on 31 May 1918 until 16 September. *The committee has not given the permission:* The Romanovs' daily schedule was regimented by the Ural Regional Executive Committee.

YEKATERINBURG 23 MAY/5 JUNE

13° WEDNESDAY

Got up at 6:30, now 8:30 by the watch.

15° Glorious morning. Baby did not sleep well, leg
25° ached probably more because Vladimir Nikolaevich took it yesterday out of the splint wh. held the knee firm. Yevgeny Sergeevich carried him
12:00–1:15. out before the house & put him in my wheeling chair & Tatiana & I sat out with him in the sun before the entry with a pailing erected around—

Back he went to bed as leg ached much fr. dressing & carrying about.

Lunch only brought at 3 o'clock.

Are putting yet higher planks before all our windows, so that not even the tops of the trees can be seen—then one will have the double windows taken out & at last we can open the windows.—

4:15. The others went out.

6:00. Vladimir Nikolaevich & Avdeev came, made him again a plaster of Paris splint as knee more swollen & hurts so again.

8:00. Supped at 8, but Baby only went to his room at 10 (8) as too light to sleep.

Played bezique—to bed at 11 (9).—

put him in my wheeling chair: From the entry for 5 June in the logbook for the special purpose detachment members on duty at the Ipatiev house: "Aleksei Romanov was taken out for a one-hour walk for the first time. During a routine examination of Aleksei Romanov by Doctor Derevenko in the presence of Commandant Avdeev, Nicholas Romanov's wife spoke German to her daughters, despite the ban on speaking foreign languages during Doctor Derevenko's visits. After which Commandant Avdeev issued a second warning" (GARF, f. 601, op. 2, d. 37, l. 1–8ob). In fact, Alexandra spoke to her daughters in English.

YEKATERINBURG 24 MAY/6 JUNE

my real B.D.

12° THURSDAY

Glorious weather.

Baby had a better night.

Lunch brought at 2:30.

25° Maria carried Baby out & put him on my basket long chair for half an hour. Olga & I sat with him, & after Nicholas & the other 3 went out into the garden. Very hot, awfully stuffy in rooms.

Vladimir Nikolaevich did not come.

Supped at 8:30 & then Baby was carried back to
12° his room.

Played a little bezique.

my real B.D.: The empress's birthday had been celebrated officially on 25 May (old style), despite the fact that at the turn of the century the difference between the old and new calendars changed from twelve to thirteen days. From Alexandra's point of view, her "real" birthday should have been celebrated on 6 June (new style).

YEKATERINBURG 25 MAY/7 JUNE

Finding of the head of the Holy Glorious Prophet, Forerunner and Baptist John

12° FRIDAY

Beautiful weather—Nicholas remains the day in bed, as slept badly two nights fr. pains—p. & better
25° when lies quietly. 12 we took Baby out with the girls, I remained ½ an hour & then Tatiana changed with me.

At 1 they had to come in again

nice breeze, very warm.

Lunch brought at 2:15. Nicholas & Aleksei had theirs in bed in our room, tea & supper too.

In the afternoon they slept a little. Nicholas 37.3°. Aleksei 36.7°.

Vladimir Nikolaevich again did not come.—

12° Nicholas felt much better in the evening, sat up a little.—Nicholas 37½°.

Nicholas began taking iodine 5 dr.

Tatiana began reading aloud to Aleksei.

The Crusaders by Sienkiewicz.—

Nicholas remains the day in bed: Nicholas suffered from hemorrhoids and rheumatism. Nicholas's diary: "I spent dear Alix's birthday in bed with strong pains in my legs and in other places!" The Crusaders *by Sienkiewicz:* A historical novel by the Polish writer Henryk Sienkiewicz, the Nobel laureate for literature in 1905.

12° SATURDAY

Grey morning, but warm.

Nicholas slept very well, without awaking. 36.6°. Baby slept nicely.

Baby was brought to us at 1.—

2:30. Lunch. Nicholas sat up til 2 & then lay down again 37.2°. Aleksei 36.1°.

Rains nearly all the afternoon. Vladimir Nikolaevich again did not come, they say as tho' there were scarlet f. in his house & that he can't come before Thursday!

Played cards with Baby. Tatiana read aloud to him

8:30. Nicholas sat up to supper near Baby's bed. After 9 (7) Aleksei was taken back to his room.

Played bezique with Nicholas, his temp. 37.2°.

Great fidgeting going on around us today, since 3 days don't give us any papers to read; & made much noise in the night.

Great fidgeting going on: The Ipatiev house guard was alarmed by the anti-Soviet mutiny of the previous day by forces of the Czechoslovak Legion, following an attempt by Communist authorities to disarm them during their evacuation to Europe on the Trans-Siberian Railroad. The ensuing local uprisings soon led to mass arrests in Yekaterinburg (see chronology).

YEKATERINBURG 27 MAY/9 JUNE

6th Sunday of Pascha (Sunday of the Blind Man)

12° SUNDAY

Glorious weather. Nicholas 36.1°.

Nicholas dressed & got up. Baby slept well.

12:00–1:00. Maria carried out Aleksei, & I sat with him, Maria, Olga & Niuta.

2:15. only lunched.

4:00–5:00. Nicholas & the others all went out into the garden—

5:30. tea. Aleksei 36.2°.

Tatiana read to Baby & me.

8:30. Supper. Played cards with him & then he was taken to his room.

Played bezique with Nicholas.

YEKATERINBURG 30 MAY/12 JUNE

11° WEDNESDAY

Raining. Baby slept well,

2:40. Lunch was only brought.

Tatiana read to us a great deal

The others all went out.

5:00. tea.

Vladimir Nikolaevich came with Avdeev but did not touch Baby as he is afraid before his quarantine is over.

8:00. Supped.

Played cards with Aleksei

9:00. He was taken back to his room.

I played bezique with Nicholas.

before his quarantine is over: Dr. Derevenko visited the Ipatiev house one day before his family's quarantine for scarlet fever was due to end.

YEKATERINBURG 31 MAY/13 JUNE

Ascension of the Lord

5° THURSDAY MY LANCERS' FEAST.

Grey morning, sunshine & rain.

Took Baby into the big room
11:30. & placed the table with the images.

12:30. They told us no Priest cld. come as such a big holiday!!

Tatiana read to us.

2:45. lunch brought.

Others told there would be no walk.—

Avdeev came & said to pack up as might have to leave any moment. Spent rest of day & whole evening packing.

At midnight Avdeev again came & said we shld. not leave before several days. Promised us Sednyov & Nagorny for Sunday, & Vladimir Nikolaevich for the journey. Said the rest of ours & Valia had left 3 days ago for Tobolsk.—

my Lancers' feast: The holiday of the Lancers regiment, whose patron Alexandra had been. *Avdeev came & said to pack up:* Nicholas's diary: "Avdeev came and talked with Yevgeny Sergeevich for a long time. According to him, he and the regional soviet are afraid of actions by anarchists, and for this reason we might have to leave quickly, probably for Moscow! He asked us to prepare for departure. We started packing at once, but quietly, at Avdeev's special request, to avoid attracting the attention of the guard officers. Around 11 o'clock at night, he returned and said that we would remain for a few more days. And so we were left sitting on our bags *for the night* and didn't unpack a thing." *Said the rest of ours & Valia had left:* Commandant Avdeev lied when he told the Romanovs that Prince Dolgorukov (Valia) had been sent to Tobolsk. Dolgorukov and Tatishchev had been summarily executed on 27 June (10 July); according to other sources, the date was 25 May (7 June).

YEKATERINBURG 1/14 JUNE

Sister Olga & Mitia's B.D.

8° FRIDAY. SOPHIE'S B.D.

Beautiful sunny weather.

12:00–1:00. Sat with Baby, Olga & Anastasia before the house. He did not sleep well.

Tatiana read to us.

2:20 lunch was brought.

The others went out.

Tatiana read again.

5:00. tea.

Vladimir Nikolaevich & Avdeev came.

8:00. supper & then Baby was taken back to his room.

Now they say we shall remain here, that they succeeded in catching the leader of the anarchists, their typography & band.

played bezique with Nicholas

always without electricity, as its so late, 11 really being 9 o'clock.—

Sister Olga & Mitia's B.D.: The birthday of Nicholas's younger sister Princess Olga Aleksandrovna and Grand Duke Dmitry Pavlovich. *Sophie's B.D.:* The birthday of Queen Sophia of Greece, wife of King Constantine I and sister of Kaiser Wilhelm II. *succeeded in catching the leader of the anarchists:* On the night of 12–13 June at the Palais-Royal Hotel in Yekaterinburg, Commissar Pavel Khokhriakov (see glossary) arrested two anarchists, one of whom put up armed resistance.

YEKATERINBURG 2/15 JUNE

11° SATURDAY

Beautiful morning, later grey & windy, but warm.

12:00–1:00. Went out with Baby, Tatiana & Maria

Tatiana read to us—

2:15. Lunched.

Others stayed in as rained.

Tatiana read to us.

Played cards with Baby.

8:00. Supper.

Continued the book.

9:00. Baby was taken to his room.

I played bezique with Nicholas.

YEKATERINBURG 3/16 JUNE

7th Sunday of Pascha

11° SUNDAY

Fine morning.

Again no service.

12:00–1:00. Sat out with Baby, Olga & Tatiana

Tatiana read to us.

2:00–5:00. Lunched.

worked (tatting.

4:00–5:00. Others walked.

Tatiana finished reading the story

Played cards with Aleksei & Yevgeny Sergeevich.

8:15. Supper.

Baby taken back & washed.

Played bezique with Nicholas.

YEKATERINBURG 4/17 JUNE

13° MONDAY

Lovely weather

Tatiana: Daniel 8–10.

12:00–1:00. Sat out with Baby, Tatiana & Anastasia

1:20 Luncheon, prepared by Kharitonov—he has to cook our food now. Worked, very hot, stuffy as no windows open & smells strong of kitchen everywhere—

Baby in my wheeling chair going about the rooms.

Man came with Avdeev to see about the windows.

Vladimir Nikolaevich & Avdeev came—

8:00. Supper.

watched Kharitonov prepare for making bread.

9:30. Baby was carried to his room.

10:30. Played bezique with Nicholas.

11:00. The girls needed the doe for the bread.

he has to cook our food now: A kitchen was set up in the Ipatiev house and the cook Kharitonov (see glossary) was permitted to prepare food for the imperial family and their retainers.

YEKATERINBURG 5/18 JUNE

Anastasia's 17th B.D.

14° TUESDAY

17° Beautiful weather. The Children continued rolling & making bread & now its baking.—

Baby was brought earlier to us.

28° Tatiana read to me *Spir. Readings*. & I worked.

1:00. Lunched—excellent bread.

3:15. Wheeled Baby into the garden & we all sat there for an hour—very hot, nice lilac bushes & small honeysuckle, quite pretty foliage, but as untidy as ever.

Rested, tired, difficult to breathe—

8:00. Supper.

Played cards with Baby—then he was taken to his room.—

Played bezique with Nicholas.

Short thunderstorm, but very stuffy in rooms.

Kind nuns send now milk & eggs for Aleksei & us & cream.

Kind nuns send now milk & eggs: Avdeev wrote in his memoirs: "The local convent petitioned for permission to contribute provisions for the Romanov family. After discussion in the regional executive committee it was decided to allow them to do this in order to keep track of the intentions of the Black Hundreds and to set up strict surveillance" (Avdeev, 202). Avdeev thus justified the committee's decision for posterity not on humanitarian grounds but for intelligence purposes.

YEKATERINBURG 6/19 JUNE

11° WEDNESDAY

Beautiful weather. 18½ in the room 9.(7.)
Worked. Tatiana read to me *Spir. Readings*—
Baby was brought to our room.
The Children help every day in the kitchen.

1:00. Luncheon.

2:50. We all went into the garden.

4:50. tea—cards, rested.

8:00. Supper.

bezique with Nicholas.

YEKATERINBURG 7/20 JUNE

Nina's 17th B.D.

10° THURSDAY

Fine weather. Baby slept well, was brought to our room at 11:30.

1:00. Luncheon, Kharitonov made a macaroni tart for the others (& me) as no meat was brought—

I cut Nicholas's hair—

2:45. We all went out for an hour into the garden

4:00. Vladimir Nikolaevich came—

4:30. tea.

Played cards, worked.

Tatiana read to me *Spir. Readings*. I had a sitting bath as cld. only bring the hot water fr. our kitchen.

4 weeks the Children came.

8:00. Supper—then Baby went to his room.

Played bezique with Nicholas & before 11 to bed as very tired.—

7 (20) June: On this day or not long before it, the first of four letters written in French by an "officer" was "illegally" delivered to the imperial family. It began: "Friends are no longer sleeping and hope that the hour so long awaited has come. . . . Be ready at every hour, day and night. . . . Answer with a few words, but, please, give all the useful information for your friends from outside" (GARF, f. 601, op. 2, d. 27, l. 27). Later the Bolsheviks produced these letters, all fabricated by the Cheka, as evidence that counterrevolutionaries were plotting an escape for Nicholas, which supposedly made his execution necessary. The surveillance file on the imperial family kept by the Ural Regional Executive Committee contains a reply presumably in Olga's hand, in French, and dated 20 June 1918: "From the corner up to the balcony there are 5 windows on the street side, 2 on the square. All of the windows are glued shut and painted white. The little one is still sick and in bed and cannot walk at all. . . . No risk whatsoever must be taken without being *absolutely* certain of the results. We are almost always under close observation" (GARF, f. 601, op. 2, d. 27, l. 270b).

YEKATERINBURG 8/21 JUNE

15° FRIDAY

19° Glorious weather.—dressed earlier as 6 women

10:00. came to wash the floors in all our rooms.

25° After that Baby came over to us.

Worked.

1:00. Lunch. Tatiana read to me *Spir. Readings*

Tought Tatiana to do tatting.

Nicholas read *Sea Stories* (Belomor) to Baby.

3:30–4:50. Out in the garden, fearfully hot, sat under the

30° bushes

they have given us still half an hour more for being out.

Vladimir Nikolaevich (never without Avdeev, so impossible to say even one word to him), came & electrified Baby's leg. His left arm is again swollen.—

Played cards with Aleksei & Yevgeny Sergeevich.

8:00. Supper.

After Baby was taken to his room, played bezique.

Thunderstorms—

Heat, airlessness in the rooms intense.

Sea Stories *(Belomor):* A book by A. Ye. Belomor found in Ipatiev's own small library.

YEKATERINBURG 9/22 JUNE

16° SATURDAY

19° Beautiful weather, in the room at 9:40 (7:40) nearly 20°.

Baby came over about 11.

1:00. Luncheon.

The others went out for an hour & a half,

3:00–4:30. Olga & I remained at home—

30° People (~~probably~~ of the commitee) came to

fr. SPb (?)* see again about the windows.

Played bezique with Baby & Yevgeny Sergeevich.

8:00. Supper—

Played bezique with Nicholas.

*Nekrasov.

(~~probably~~ of the committee): The word *probably* was crossed out and *fr. Spb.* (St. Petersburg) added in the margin the next day.

YEKATERINBURG 10/23 JUNE

Day of the Holy Trinity

13° SUNDAY

Glorious weather—Went with Tatiana to Yevgeny Sergeevich who had kidney pains & she made hm an injection of morphia, suffers very much since 6 in the moring—lies in bed.

Two of the soldiers came & took out one window in our room, such joy, delicious air at last & one window no longer whitewashed.

11:30. Had the great blessing of a real *obednitsa* & vespers, first since 3 months—simply on the table with all our images & lots of birchtree branches. The first old Priest officiated.—20½° in the room.

1:00. Luncheon. Yevgeny Sergeevich still feels bad, was sick, sat with him, Tatiana & I remained in, the
3:00. others went out (now may be out 2 hours).—

After tea Vladimir Nikolaevich came.—

Yevgeny Sergeevich went over again into the big room, as more air & quieter, Niuta will again be in the dining room.

8:00. Supped, with all, Baby too,—

then the others wheeled him about through the rooms.

Tatiana sleeps with Aleksei.

Played bezique with Nicholas & Yevgeny Sergeevich in bed bridge with the girls.

The first old Priest officiated: Anatoly Grigorievich Meledin.

YEKATERINBURG 11/24 JUNE

Day of the Holy Spirit

13° MONDAY

Window open all night, good air, but so noisy.—
19½° in the room!

Baby since the morning wheeled about. Yevgeny Sergeevich slept well, better.

1:00. Lunched in our room, Aleksei on the straw lounge.

37½° in the sun, 21½° in the room.

In the morning all & Baby went out for half an hour, Yevgeny Sergeevich remained in bed; I on the bed as much as possible as heart enlarged.

3:00. All went out, only Marie stayed with me, I lay near the window reading & she played cards near his bed,

6:00. Vladimir Nikolaevich came—

8:00. Dined with all—

36½°. Masséed Baby's leg & put on his compress, Tatiana sleeps with him.

I went to bed at 10, 22½° in the room & 21° outside.

Window open all night: Between 20 and 25 June the imperial family received a second letter from the "officer": "With the help of God and your sangfroid we hope to succeed without taking any risk. One of your windows must be unglued so that you can open it at the right time. Indicate which window, please" (GARF, f. 601. op. 2. d. 27. l. 27). The window may have been kept open all night deliberately in response to this letter.

YEKATERINBURG 12/25 JUNE

16° TUESDAY

At 8:30 16° in the shade, 21° in the room.

Baby slept well, was wheeled about through the rooms. Yevgeny Sergeevich had a good night, still in bed as feels week & all aches when gets up.

1:00. Luncheon.

2:30. All went out, Tatiana remained with me, read *Spir. Readings* & then Daniel 16– to the end. & Hosea 1–5.

8:00. Supper.

12 (25) June: On this day the imperial family replied to the second letter from the "officer."

YEKATERINBURG 13/26 JUNE

WEDNESDAY

Very hot again. 22½° in the room. Arranged things.

1:00. Lunched, Baby in his wheeling chair & Yevgeny Sergeevich for the first time up, in an armchair à 3 in our bedroom.

2:30–4:30. They went out. Olga stayed with me.

Yevgeny Sergeevich sat with us.

4:30. tea—Vladimir Nikolaevich came—

8:00. Supper like we lunched. Baby sleeps tonight in our room—more air for him, & to have him nearer, & Tatiana's bed is back in its old place—Colossal heat tho' rained a little in the day. I went early to bed, but slept only 3 hours, as they made so much noise outside.

13 (26) June: Between 12 (25) and 14 (27) June the imperial family received the third letter from the "officer": "Hoping before Sunday to indicate the detailed plan of the operation. As of now it is like this: once the signal comes, you close and barricade with furniture the door that separates you from the guards, who will be blocked and terror-stricken inside the house. With a rope especially made for that purpose, you climb out through the window—we will be waiting for you at the bottom. The rest is not difficult" (GARF, f. 601, op. 2, d. 27, l. 24).

YEKATERINBURG 14/27 JUNE

Marie's 19th B.D.

17° THURSDAY

Early morning 22° in the room.

Arranged things all day, tatted, Yevgeny Sergeevich sat with me often, as can sit up now; Baby wheeled about.

1:00. Lunched; then the others went out, Olga remained with me—

Vladimir Nikolaevich did not come, but again the Military Commissar & Chairman of the Committee to look through the rooms, wont open another window, so Kharitonov & little Sednyov will sleep in Baby's room, being less hot than theirs near the kitchen. Heat intense

8:00. Supper. 23° in the room,

Scarcely slept.

Scarcely slept: Drafted by Pyotr Voikov (see the glossary) and Aleksandr Beloborodov and copied over in French by the Chekist Isai Rodzinsky, the letters from the "officer" were a concerted effort to provoke the imperial family to attempt an escape from the Ipatiev house. Their response to the third letter was unambiguously negative: "We do not want to, nor can we, *escape*. We can only be *carried off* by force, just as it was force that was used to carry us from Tobolsk. . . . If you are watching over us, you can always come save us *in case of* real and imminent danger. We are completely unaware of what is going on outside, for we receive no magazines, newspapers or letters. Since we have been allowed to open the window, the surveillance has increased, and we are forbidden even to stick our heads out, at the risk of getting shot in the face" (GARF, f. 601, op. 2, d. 27, l. 24). A sentry fired in Anastasia's direction one day when she dared to poke her head out the window. The bullet hit the window frame.

19° FRIDAY

At 8:30 (6:30) already 23½° in the room, later over 24°.—Tatted—

1:00. Lunched in our room.

2:30–4:30. the others went out, Olga stayed with me—

4:30. tea.

Vladimir Nikolaevich came—

8:00. Supped with Baby—

All went earlier to bed as very tired & heat intense—24½° room—

In the sun in the morning there were 30 dgs.

We hear the night sentry under our rooms being told quite particularly to watch every movement at our window—they have become again most suspicious since our window is opened & don't allow one to sit on the sill even now.

they have become again most suspicious: The Ural Regional Executive Committee had permitted the window in the Ipatiev house to be opened. However, the Ipatiev house guards answered for the imperial family with their lives and reacted warily to the apparent easing of their charges' regime.

YEKATERINBURG 16/29 JUNE

14° SATURDAY

Very hot day again. Tatted.

arranged things. Scarcely slept—

1:00. Lunched.

3:00–5:00. The others went out, Maria remained with me—.

Arranged medicines with Yevgeny Sergeevich—

5:00. tea—busy—

8:00. Supper.

Military Commissar looked in to see if we were all there.

I dont go out because of the heat & my heart—

YEKATERINBURG 17/30 JUNE

16° SUNDAY

Slept barely 4 hours, the sentry made so much noise. Alas cant have service. Arranged things, tatted, heart enlarged.

1:00. Lunched.

3:00–5:00. The others went out, Anastasia remained with me.

6:00. Vladimir Nikolaevich came.

8:00. Supper.

Played a little bezique & early again to bed.

Very heavy rain, cooler night.

YEKATERINBURG 18 JUNE/1 JULY

Beginning of St. Peter Fast

12° MONDAY ALL SAINTS' WEEK

20° in the room, rather grey.—

Much fresher air, whole day lovely breeze into our room. Arranged things.

1:00. Lunched.

3:00–5:00. Others walked, Marie remained with me—

Read & tatted.

8:00. Supped. bezique

10:30. went to bed.

Beginning of St. Peter Fast. The fast of Saints Peter and Paul lasted two weeks.

12° TUESDAY

Beautiful morning.

Spent the day as usual.

In the morning the others went out ½ hour in the afternoon 1½—

Tatiana stayed with me.—

Arranged things, tatted, read. Vladimir Nikolaevich came.

1:00. Lunched, 8 supped.

To bed at 11.

Now Avdeev has to come morning & evening to see if we are all there.

In the daytime came to-day to ask if I don't go out because of my health, seems committee wont believe it.—

Bezique.—

YEKATERINBURG 20 JUNE/3 JULY

14° WEDNESDAY

Again glorious weather, yet warmer—20° in the room at 9.

Everything as yesterday.

Tatiana stopped with me in the morning when they went out, & Olga in the afternoon, played bezique together—Baby begins makig movements with his leg. Very hot & airless.—

Before supper Maria & Niuta washed my head.

10:30. I took a bath—

In the night strong rain & thunderstorm.

YEKATERINBURG 21 JUNE/4 JULY

16° THURSDAY

Very hot, 21½° in the room at 9.

During lunch the chairman of the Regional Committee came with some men, Avdeev is being changed & we get a new commandant (who came over to look at Baby's leg, & another time our rooms) with a young help who seems decent whereas the other vulgar & unpleasant

All our guard of inside left (probably one found out that they had been steeling our things out of the shed).—Both men then made us show all our jewels we had on, & the young one wrote them all down in detail & then they were taken from us (where to, for how long, why?? don't know.) only left me my two bracelets of U. Leo's wh. I cant take off, & the children 1 bracelet each wh. we gave & can't be removed, neither Nicholas's engagement cld. he get off.—

So the others only got out from 6–7. Olga remained with me.

They took all our kees wh. one had left us of the boxes in the hall, but promised to return them.

Very hot, went early to bed as awfully tired & heart ached more.

we get a new commandant . . . with a young help: Avdeev was dismissed for theft of the imperial family's belongings by his subordinates and replaced by the Chekists Yakov Yurovsky and his aide Grigory Nikulin. *All our guard of inside left:* Yurovsky immediately tightened discipline and security at the Ipatiev house, and replaced the entire internal guard with handpicked, largely foreign Communists. *Both men then made us show all our jewels:* Yurovsky wrote in his memoirs that he and Nikulin confiscated the family's jewelry lest it tempt members of the guard, and that at Nicholas's request he left Aleksei his watch. After indignant protests from Alexandra, he allowed her and her daughters to keep gold bracelets that could not be removed without tools. *U. Leo:* Possibly Uncle Leo.

13° FRIDAY

Spent the day as usual.

The command. came with our jewels, before us sealed them up & left them on our table & will come every day to see that we have not opened the packet.—

22 June (5 July): On this day novices from the Novotikhvinsky Convent brought provisions for the imperial family to the Ipatiev house. The imperial family also received its fourth and last letter from the "officer."

YEKATERINBURG 23 JUNE/6 JULY

Toria's 50 B.D.

10° SATURDAY

Sunny with clouds, several showers during the day.

Two woman came & washed the floors. The others walked in the afternoon, Anastasia remained with me—

Played cards with Baby & Yevgeny Sergeevich after tea.

The Command. brought Nicholas his watch in leather case wh. he found in the service room stolen out of Nicholas's trunk.—

Played bezique.

Had a bath.

Command. is called Yurovsky.

Toria's 50 B.D.: Birthday of Princess Victoria, Nicholas's and Alexandra's English cousin. *The others walked in the afternoon:* During the imperial family's walks, Yurovsky and his aide watched to make sure that the guards had no contact with the Romanovs. Some guards were dismissed for conversing with the prisoners. *The Command. brought Nicholas his watch in leather case:* Nicholas's diary: "Yesterday Commandant Yurovsky brought a little box containing all our jewelry, asked that we check the contents and sealed it in our presence, leaving it with us for safekeeping. . . . Yurovsky and his aide are beginning to understand *what sort of* people were surrounding and guarding us, while stealing us blind. Never mind our belongings, they were even keeping for themselves most of the supplies brought from the convent. We have only learned about this now, after the change [in commandants], because the whole amount of provisions has begun reaching the kitchen."

YEKATERINBURG 24 JUNE/7 JULY

1st Sunday after All Saints

8° SUNDAY IVAN KUPALA

Lovely morning, in the sun quite warm, in the shade only 8° at 8:30. Spent the day as usual. In the afternoon I went out with the others for the first time, since a good while. Nice air, not too hot. In the morning Yevgeny Sergeevich went out for the first time.

In the evening there was a thunderstorm tho' the air was quite cool—& it poured.

Still no Vladimir Nikolaevich came.

Ivan Kupala: East Slavic folk holiday with pagan roots in the celebration of the summer solstice, coinciding with the Nativity of John the Baptist.

10° MONDAY

Cooler—nothing particular happened. The others went out for ½ hour in the morning & 1½ in the afternoon, Maria remained at home with me.

Fine & yet a few showers. Lunched only at 1:30, because they were arranging the electricity in our rooms, Tatiana even did my hair whilst they were working.—

Still no Vladimir Nikolaevich tho' we daily ask for him.—

Baby eats well & is getting heavy for the others to carry, cruel they wont give us Nagorny back again. He moves his leg easier when making movements with Yevgeny Sergeevich, after massage.—

Played bezique.

Poured in the night.—

YEKATERINBURG 26 JUNE/9 JULY

10° TUESDAY

Day passed as usual.

They went out twice, Olga stayed with me. Several showers. Still no Vladimir Nikolaevich.—Tatted, layed patiences, dont read more than 5 m. because of eyes wh. still ache. Played cards with Baby & Yevgeny Sergeevich & bezique with Nicholas.

Arsenic.

11° WEDNESDAY

Sunny morning.

3:00–4:30. Went out in the afternoon with the others, ideal weather;—very strong back & leg ache fr. kidneys probably.

2 day the others have no meat & live upon Kharitonov's Tobolsk remaining meagre provisions.

Took a bath.

bezique. They still find excuses not to bring Vladimir Nikolaevich

YEKATERINBURG 28 JUNE/11 JULY

Irenes B.D. 52

12° THURSDAY

The Ox Command. insisted to see us all at 10, but kept us waiting 20 m. as was breakfasting & eating cheese

wont permit us to have any more any cream.

10:30. Workmen turned up outside & began putting up iron railings before our only open window. Always fright of our climbing out no doubt or getting into contact with the sentry. Strong pains continue. Greyish weather.

Brought me for 6 days, but so little only suffices for putting in the soup.

The Bull very rude to Kharitonov.

Remained in bed all day. Lunched only, as they brought the meat so late.—Anastasia read to me whilst the others went out. Lovely weather.

Irenes B.D. 52: The birthday of Alexandra's sister Irene, wife of Prince Heinrich of Prussia. *The Ox Command.:* The prisoners' nickname for Yurovsky. *Workmen began putting up iron railings:* Nicholas's diary: "Around 10:30 in the morning, three workers came to the open window, lifted a heavy grating and attached it to the outside of the window frame without any warning from Yurovsky. We are starting to like this character less and less!" *Brought me:* Meat was delivered. *The Bull:* Probably also refers to Yurovsky.

YEKATERINBURG 29 JUNE/12 JULY

Holy Apostles Peter and Paul

13° FRIDAY

Bright sunshine—in the afternoon then were severel showers & short thunderstorms.

The others went out twice,—Maria remained with me, I spent the day on my bed & got into it again at 9:30. Lovely evening. Every day one of the girls reads to me *Spir. Readings,* i.e. *Complete Yearly Cycle of Brief Homilies for Each Day of the Year* (Grig. Diachenko).—

Constantly hear artillery passing, infantry & twice cavalry during the course of this week. Also troops marching with music—twice it seems to have been the Austrian prisoners who are marching against the Chechs (also our former prisoners) who are with the troops coming through Siberia & not far fr. here now. Wounded daily arrive to the town.—

Constantly hear artillery passing: Yekaterinburg was in a state of siege. More and more fighting units, some consisting of volunteers (German and Austrian former prisoners of war), were being sent from the city to fight the rapidly advancing Czechs and White Guards. The Executive Committee of the Ural Regional Soviet met on this date and resolved to execute the Romanovs without trial (see chronology).

YEKATERINBURG 30 JUNE/13 JULY

Louise's 29 B.D.

11° SATURDAY

Beautiful morning. I spent the day as yesterday lying on the bed, as back aches when move about.

Others went out twice. Anastasia remained with me in the afternoon. One says Nagorny & Sednyov have been sent out of this government, instead of giving them back to us.—

At 6:30 Baby had his first bath since Tobolsk. He managed to get in & out alone, climbs also alone in & out of bed, but can only stand on one foot as yet. 9:45 I went to bed again.—

Rained in the night.

Heard three revolver shots in the night.

Louise's 29 B.D.: Birthday of Princess Louise of Battenberg, Alexandra's niece. *One says Nagorny & Sednyov have been sent out of this government:* By *government* Alexandra evidently meant Perm government territory, which included Yekaterinburg. Nagorny and Sednyov had by now been executed. *Baby had his first bath since Tobolsk:* Yurovsky recalled that the imperial family "took no small pleasure in rinsing themselves off in the bath several times a day. However, I forbade them to do this often, since there was a water shortage" (Iurovskii, 111).

YEKATERINBURG 1/14 JULY

12° SUNDAY

Beautiful summers morning.

Scarcely slept because of back & legs.

10:30. Had the joy of an *obednitsa*—the young Priest for the 2nd time

11:30–12:00. The others walked—Olga with me.

Spend the day on the bed again

Tatiana stayed with me in the afternoon.

Spir. Readings, Book of the Prophet Hosea, ch. 4–14, Pr. Joel 1– the end.

4:30. tea—tatted all day & laid patiences. Played a little bezique in the eveing, they put my long straw couch in the big room so it was less tiring for me.

10:00. Took a bath—& went to bed.

Had the joy of an obednitsa*—the young Priest for the 2nd time:* Fr. Storozhev and Deacon Buimirov were summoned to officiate again at the Ipatiev house. Both felt that "something had happened" to the Romanovs: for the first time no one in the family had sung during services (Ross, 101).

YEKATERINBURG 2/15 JULY

4th Week of Pentecost

11° MONDAY MARIE E.'S B.D.

Greyish morning. Later sunshine. Lunched on the couch in the big room, as women came to clean the floors, then lay on my bed again & read with Maria J. Sirach 26–31. They went out twice as usual. In the morning Tatiana read to me *Spir. Readings*. Still no Vladimir Nikolaevich—at 6:30 Baby had his second bath—Bezique. Went to bed 10:15.—

11¼° of warmth at 10:30 evening.

Heard the report of an artillery shot in the night & several revolver shots.

Women came to clean the floors: Two women, Maria Starodumova and Vassa Driagina, later testified that they had found the family in the upper quarters, playing cards, while Yurovsky sat opposite Aleksei, asking about his health: "Yurovsky was courteous, but he didn't allow us to talk with the imperial family, who were all in a good mood; the duchesses were laughing, and there was no sadness about them" (Ross, 82).

YEKATERINBURG 3/16 JULY

Irina's 23rd B.D.

11° TUESDAY

Grey morning, later lovely sunshine. Baby has a slight cold. All went out ½ hour in the morning, Olga & I arranged our medicines. Tatiana read

3:00. *Spir. Readings*. They went out, Tatiana stayed with me & we read: Bk. of the Pr. Amos and Pr. Obadiah. Tatted. Every moring the Command. comes to our rooms, at last after a week brought eggs again for Baby.

8:00. Supper.

Suddenly Lyonka Sednyov was fetched to go & see his Uncle & flew off—wonder whether its true & we shall see the boy back again!

Played bezique with Nicholas.

10:30. to bed. 15 degrees.

Irina's 23rd B.D.: Birthday of Princess Irina Aleksandrovna, the daughter of Nicholas's sister Grand Duchess Ksenia Aleksandrovna and Grand Duke Aleksandr Mikhailovich. *Olga & I arranged our medicines:* Alexandra and Olga completed reconstructing the corsets concealing densely packed diamonds that Alexandra and her daughters were wearing when they were executed that night. *brought eggs again for Baby:* Eggs, milk, and thread were delivered from the convent. *Lyonka Sednyov was fetched:* The fourteen-year-old kitchen boy, Leonid Sednyov (see glossary).

4/17 JULY

WEDNESDAY

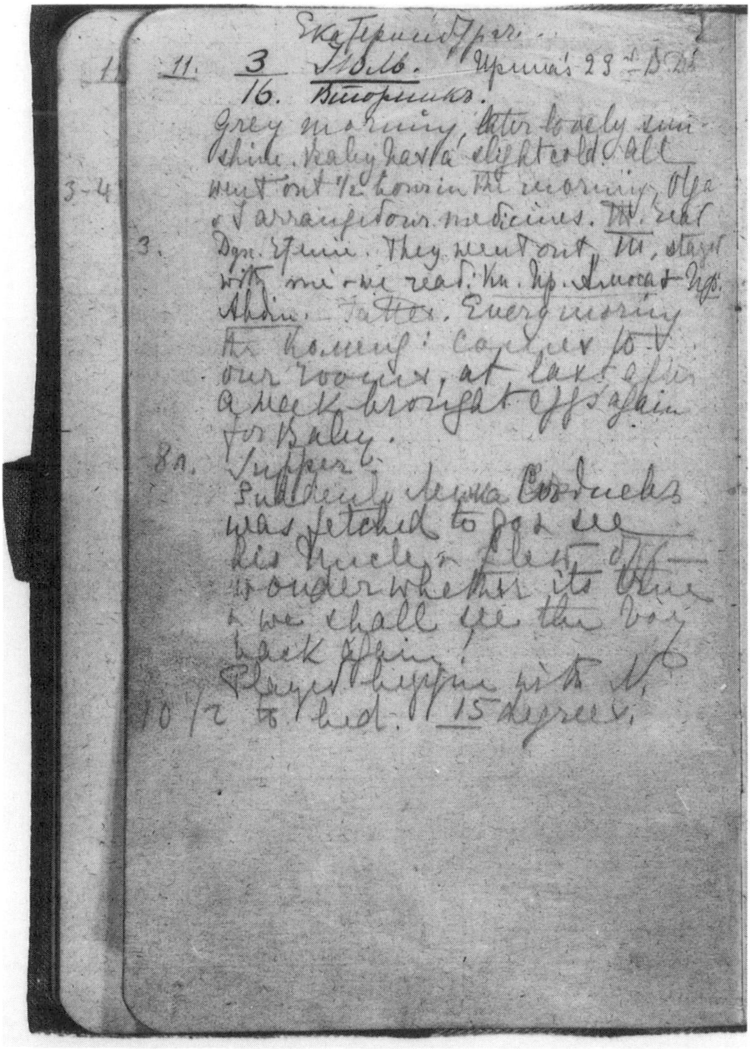
11. 3/16 [illegible] [illegible] 23 [illegible]
Grey morning, later lovely sunshine. Baby has a slight cold. All went out 1/2 hour in the morning, Olga & I arranged our medicines. T. read [illegible]. They went out, T. stayed with me & we read: [illegible]. Tatted. Every morning the Komendant comes to our rooms, at last after a week brought eggs again for Baby.
8 p. Supper.
Suddenly [illegible] was fetched to go & see his Uncle & flew off — wonder whether its true & we shall see the boy back again!
Played bezique with N.
10 1/2 to bed. 15 degrees.

Alexandra's last diary entry, 3 (16) July 1918.

94

4\. Июль.

17\. Среда.

Afterword: The Diaries of Alexandra

Vladimir A. Kozlov and
Vladimir M. Khrustalëv

ON THE NIGHT OF 16–17 July 1918 in the city of Yekaterinburg in the Urals, the Bolsheviks executed the last Russian emperor, Nicholas II, and his family. Three days later, *Pravda,* the leading Bolshevik newspaper, reported that the Central Executive Committee (VTsIK) had in its possession "extremely important material and documents of Nicholas II: his handwritten diaries which he had kept from his youth until recent times, the diaries of his wife and children, the Romanov correspondence, etc. Among the items are also letters from Grigory Rasputin to Romanov and his family. All of these materials will be studied and published in the very near future." In fact, at this time the intimate documents of the imperial couple, their children, and their suite had not yet been transferred from the Urals. It was not until the night of 19–20 July 1918 that Yakov Yurovsky, who had organized the murder of the Romanovs, departed for Moscow, taking with him "seven pieces of luggage." The coachman who drove Yurovsky to the train station saw among his things two leather traveling bags, one of which was sealed with wax.

The full text of Alexandra's 1918 diary is published here for the first time; it has been prepared from the handwritten original stored in the State Archive as f. R-640, op. 1, d. 326. Documents of the former Central Party Archive of the Institute of Marxism-Leninism (now the Russian Center for the Preservation and Study of Documents of Recent History [RTsKhIDNI]) and the former KGB archives (now the Central Archive of the Russian Federal Security Service [TsAFSBRF]) indicate that the imperial couple's diaries were turned in to the People's Commissariat of Internal Affairs (NKVD) in Moscow and that at least some were passed on to the Presidium of the VTsIK. Only the most important of Nicholas's and Alexandra's personal documents reached Moscow. A hasty evacuation (the Whites were advancing on Yekaterinburg) forced the Chekists to leave a significant portion of the belongings and papers of the Romanovs and their retinue in a bank storeroom. Some of these papers, personal effects, and jewels disappeared, owing to theft by the guards or other causes. The Whites, and subsequently the Bolsheviks, managed to find certain items. In the 1920s, documents of the Romanovs, including documents transferred from Yekaterinburg, ended up in government storage in the Central Archive and, after its reorganization, in the Central State Archive of Ancient Documents (TsGADA) of the Soviet Union (now the Russian State Archive of Ancient Documents [RGADA]), and later in the Central State Archive of the October Revolution (TsGAOR) (now the State Archive of the Russian Federation [GARF]).

Among the documents Yurovsky delivered to Moscow were the personal diaries of the last Russian empress, Alexandra Fyodorovna. These diaries are currently kept in the collection of personal papers of Alexandra Fyodorovna (GARF, fond R-640). The file for collection 640 vaguely mentions the loss of some of her diaries. The first disappearances (the diaries for 1893, 1895, and 1896) were registered in a document dated 4 June 1953. It states that these diaries were first reported missing during the first audit of the collection in 1945. The authors of this document imply that the documents disappeared during evacuation to the city of Orsk, "where the safeguarding of documentary materials was not adequately provided for." In January 1991, the 1898 diary could not be found, nor could a memo book from 1916. Only their file folders remained. The archive staff checking the presence of the documents suggested that during previous audits (in 1948 and

1953), these empty folders must have been inventoried as standard files, while the documents they had once contained had been lost during the evacuation. In 1991 yet another document was drawn up, which, while lacking legal weight, indicated that an archive employee had been responsible for the loss of Alexandra's 1917 diary. Officially this diary is not listed as missing; it has been in the card catalog of the search department since 1988 and has yet to be struck from the register. Fortunately, in 1923 an archive copyist made copies of Alexandra Fyodorovna's last diaries, for the years 1916–1918.

Thus, the State Archive of the Russian Federation currently houses ten of Alexandra Fyodorovna's diaries (either the original or copies): for the years 1887 through 1892, 1894, and for the years 1916 through 1918. The 1887 "diary" is a blank small-format notebook with a dedication in German (the inventory erroneously indicates "English language"); the entries in the 1894 diary break off at 11 May. The diaries for 1899 through 1915 are not in the archive, and its records contain no information about their fate. (In all likelihood they were never deposited there for storage.) Unfortunately, we also do not know precisely how many diaries Yurovsky transferred from Yekaterinburg to Moscow in July 1918. It is not even certain whether the empress kept diaries during this "gap" period. It is possible, though not very likely, that whatever diaries existed for 1899 through 1915 stayed in the Urals and were lost there. Or perhaps Alexandra destroyed them herself in 1917. Her diary entries after 8 March 1917 mention the burning of letters and papers, and Alexandra's closest friend, Anna Vyrubova, wrote in her memoirs of the destruction "of *all* letters and diaries dear to her" (italics ours) lest they "fall into the hands of evil-doers."

The notion of publishing Alexandra's diary first appeared a few years after her death. On 10 September 1918 the Presidium of the VTsIK established a committee "to study the materials belonging to the last Romanov." During this period excerpts from Nicholas's diaries and the imperial family's correspondence began appearing in the Soviet press, including *Pravda* and *Izvestiia*. In 1923 an unknown copyist made handwritten copies of the notebooks for 1916 and 1917. He was able to decipher most of the text, with occasional mistakes; however, the work progressed no further. Publication of the diaries was rejected, probably for chiefly ideological and political reasons. Alexandra's diary too clearly contradicted the Soviet ideological clichés that had already formed concerning the last Russian empress's cast of mind. Nonetheless, the copyist's work in the end proved very useful. It is only from the copies made in the twenties that we are able to judge the contents of the 1917 diary.

In the twenties, archivists published a number of items from the Romanov dynasty's legacy of manuscripts, including a multivolume edition, *Perepiska Nikolaia I Aleksandry Romanovykh. 1915–1917* (The correspondence of Nicholas and Alexandra Romanov, 1915–1917) (Moscow–Leningrad, 1923–25) and a magazine version of Nicholas's diaries in *Krasnyi arkhiv* (Red archive) in 1927.

Alexandra's last diaries have thus never before been published in full. American journalist Isaac Don Levine first published excerpts from the 1918 diary in the *Chicago Daily News* (22–26, 28 June 1920) from photocopies given to him by historian Mikhail Pokrovsky in November 1919. Levine later reproduced these excerpts in his autobiography *Eyewitness to History* (New York, 1963). Richard Pipes quoted from these in his book *The Russian Revolution* (New York, 1990). These excerpts match the original diaries kept in the State Archive.

Chronology
1 (14) January–18 July 1918

1 (14) January: Attempt to assassinate Lenin.

29 January (12 February): The Sovnarkom (Council of People's Commissars) discusses transferring former emperor Nicholas II to Petrograd for trial.

1 (14) February: The Gregorian calendar is officially adopted in Soviet Russia.

20 February: The Sovnarkom revisits the issue of trying Nicholas II. The People's Commissariat of Justice is charged with preparing investigative materials, and the issue of transferring Nicholas is postponed pending clarification of the case.

23 February: The authorities in Tobolsk are informed of the curtailment of the government's allowance for maintaining the imperial family in Siberian exile.

3 March: At Brest-Litovsk, Russia agrees to peace terms with Germany that Lenin describes as "obscene" but necessary. Treaty provokes widespread dissent in party and society.

1 April: The Presidium of the All-Russian Central Executive Committee (VTsIK) adopts a secret resolution calling for the evacuation of the imperial family from Tobolsk to Moscow.

6 April: The Presidium of the VTsIK adopts a new resolution to transfer the Romanovs to Yekaterinburg in the Urals rather than to Moscow.

9 April: Chairman of the Presidium of the VTsIK Yakov Sverdlov writes a letter to the Executive Committee of the Ural Regional

Soviet putting Extraordinary Commissar Vasily Yakovlev in charge of evacuating the imperial family from Tobolsk to Yekaterinburg and confining the former tsar under a strict security regime pending further orders from Moscow.

23 April: Yakovlev pays his first visit to the imperial family in the Governor's House in Tobolsk.

24 April: Yakovlev receives a wire from Sverdlov agreeing to the transfer of only Nicholas and part of the imperial family out of Tobolsk, due to tsarevich Aleksei's illness.

25 April: Yakovlev informs the imperial family of the Sovnarkom's decision to evacuate Nicholas from Tobolsk but does not reveal the ultimate destination.

26 April: Before dawn, Yakovlev and his armed detachment take Nicholas, Alexandra, their daughter Maria, Dr. Botkin, Nicholas's aide Vasily Dolgorukov, and three servants in horse-drawn carriages at high speed from Tobolsk to the railroad junction of Tiumen, where a special train awaits them.

27 April: The imperial family reaches Tiumen in the late evening and boards the train. Yakovlev wires Sverdlov and obtains approval to reverse the train's direction from west (to Yekaterinburg) to east (to Omsk) in order to avoid assassination attempts by Ural Red Guard detachments.

28 April: His train detained near Omsk, Yakovlev negotiates by wire with Moscow and is ordered to reverse direction again and ride on with his charges to Yekaterinburg.

30 April: The imperial family detrains at Yekaterinburg and settles in the Ipatiev house. Dolgorukov, however, is arrested and imprisoned.

18 May: A Central Committee plenum resolves not to take any measures "regarding Nicholas II" for the time being.

23 May: The rest of the family and suite are delivered to Yekaterinburg by Commissar Pavel Khokhriakov. Several retainers are arrested, and most are not permitted to reside with the family in the Ipatiev house.

25 May: Forces of the Czechoslovak Legion mutiny following an attempt by Bolshevik authorities—pressured by Germany—to disarm them during their evacuation eastward by the Trans-Siberian Railroad. The Czechoslovak Legion of approximately 35,000 Czech and Slovak former prisoners of war and defectors from the Austro-Hungarian army quickly occupies a number of cities along the rail route in the Volga region, the

Urals, and Siberia. Martial law is declared in Yekaterinburg. On 25 July the White Czechoslovak forces will take the city.

7–8 June: The Czechoslovak Legion takes Samara, which becomes the seat of an anti-Bolshevik Socialist Revolutionary government of former Constituent Assembly deputies.

10 June: An anti-Soviet rebellion in Yekaterinburg is attempted by members of the "Union of Front-Line Soldiers" and many peasant sympathizers. The rally is dispersed and the ringleaders arrested. Martial law in the city is intensified; mass searches and arrests begin.

Night of 12–13 June: In Perm, Chekists secretly kidnap and execute Grand Duke Mikhail Aleksandrovich (Nicholas's brother) and his English secretary, Nicholas Johnson. At the Palais-Royal Hotel in Yekaterinburg, Khokhriakov arrests two anarchists, which provokes open rebellion against the Bolsheviks.

13 June: Aleksandr Avdeev, commandant of the Ipatiev house, tells the imperial family "in secret" that the anarchists' actions might require that the family depart quickly. However, the anarchists surrender, never having contemplated rescuing the imperial family. Avdeev's "warning" was a provocation.

22 June: Front commander Reingold Berzin visits the Ipatiev house and wires Moscow that rumors that Nicholas has been killed are false.

23 June: Conservatives and monarchists form an anti-Bolshevik Provisional Government of Autonomous Siberia in Omsk.

4 July: Chairman of the Executive Committee of the Ural Regional Soviet Aleksandr Beloborodov wires Chairman Sverdlov of the VTsIK and Filipp Goloshchekin about the replacement of Avdeev and the internal guards at the Ipatiev house. Yakov Yurovsky is the new commandant.

6 July: During the Fifth All-Russian Congress of Soviets, Left Socialist Revolutionaries attempt a rebellion in Moscow.

7 July: The Soviet government suppresses the rebellion of Left Socialist Revolutionaries. Mass arrests ensue. An anti-Bolshevik uprising in the Volga port city of Yaroslavl continues through 21 July.

12 July: The Executive Committee of the Ural Regional Soviet, citing the imminent fall of Yekaterinburg to the Whites, moves to execute the Romanovs without conducting the trial of Nicholas II that Moscow planned. Yurovsky is entrusted with the execution and the disposal of bodies.

16 July: Head of the Petrograd Soviet Grigory Zinoviev relays to Lenin and Sverdlov at the Kremlin a wire received from the Ural Regional Executive Committee stating the need to decide the fate of the imperial family quickly, in view of the military situation.

Night of 16–17 July: In Yekaterinburg the imperial family, along with Dr. Botkin, Demidova, Kharitonov, and Trupp, are killed in the Ipatiev house basement by Yurovsky and his execution squad.

17 July: The Executive Committee of the Ural Regional Soviet wires Sverdlov and Lenin in the Kremlin that Nicholas has been executed. At around nine in the evening Lenin and Sverdlov receive an encoded telegram from the same Executive Committee confirming the execution of the entire imperial family along with the former tsar. Only the execution of Nicholas is announced in the press on 19 July.

Night of 17–18 July: Near Alapaevsk, in the Urals, the Cheka executes the empress's sister Grand Duchess Yelizaveta Fyodorovna, together with Grand Duke Sergei Mikhailovich, Princes Ioann Konstantinovich, Konstantin Konstantinovich, and Igor Konstantinovich Romanov, Prince Vladimir Pavlovich Palei, and two retainers.

18 July: The Presidium of the VTsIK passes a resolution approving the decision and actions of the Executive Committee of the Ural Regional Soviet in executing Nicholas.

Glossary

Accent marks indicate stressed syllables in Russian names.

Aleksándr Mikháilovich (Sandro) (1866–1933). Grand duke, great-uncle and brother-in-law of Nicholas II, husband of Grand Duchess Ksenia Aleksandrovna, adjutant general in the imperial suite, vice admiral. After his discharge on 22 March 1917, lived in exile on his estate Ai-Todor in the Crimea with his family and the dowager empress, Maria Fyodorovna.

Alekséi Nikoláevich (Baby, Little One, Sunbeam) (1904–1918). Tsarevich (heir to the throne), son of Nicholas II and Alexandra. Hemophiliac. Executed together with his family in Yekaterinburg on the night of 16–17 July 1918.

Alexander II (Aleksándr Nikoláevich) (1818–1881). Emperor of Russia 1855–1881, grandfather of Nicholas II, assassinated on 1 March 1881 by members of the People's Will (Narodnaia Volia), an organization of radical populists.

Alexander III (Aleksándr Aleksándrovich) (1845–1894). Emperor of Russia 1881–1894, father of Nicholas II.

Alexandra (Aleksándra) Fyódorovna (Alix) (1872–1918). Born in Darmstadt as Alix Victoria Helena Louise Beatrice, princess of Hesse-Darmstadt, granddaughter of Queen Victoria. In 1894 she converted from Lutheranism to Russian Orthodoxy in order to marry Nicholas II, becoming Grand Duchess Alexandra Fyodorovna. Crowned empress in 1896. Executed together with her family in Yekaterinburg on the night of 16–17 July 1918.

Anastasía Nikoláevna (1901–1918). Grand duchess, fourth daughter of Nicholas II and Alexandra Fyodorovna. Executed together with her family in Yekaterinburg on the night of 16–17 July 1918.

Ania, Anna. See Vyrubova, Anna Aleksándrovna.

Avdéev, Aleksándr Dmítrievich. Factory worker in Yekaterinburg, political exile, Bolshevik. Member of the Executive Committee of the Ural Regional Soviet. Took part in transferring Nicholas II from Tobolsk to Yekaterinburg. Commandant of the Ipatiev house, where the imperial family was imprisoned. Dismissed on 4 July 1918 and sent to the front.

Baby. See Alekséi Nikoláevich.

Beloboródov, Aleksándr Geórgievich (1891–1939). Ural factory worker. Bolshevik from 1907. Became chairman of the Ural Regional Soviet in January 1918 and helped to organize the execution of the Romanovs.

Bítner, Klávdia Mikháilovna (b. 1878). Former director of the Mariinsky women's gymnasium (secondary school) in Tsarskoe Selo. Tutored the imperial children while they were in Tobolsk. Later married Yevgeny Kobylinsky.

Bótkin, Yevgény Sergéevich (1865–1918). Personal doctor of Nicholas II and his family. Joined the Romanovs as a voluntary prisoner in Tobolsk and Yekaterinburg. Executed with the family on the night of 16–17 July 1918.

Buksgévden (Buxhoeveden), Sófia Kárlovna (Isa) (1884–1956). Baroness, lady-in-waiting to Alexandra. Voluntarily followed the imperial family to Tobolsk and accompanied the imperial children to Yekaterinburg, but was not allowed to reside with the family.

Central Executive Committee of Soviets of Workers', Peasants', and Red Army Deputies, All-Russian (VTsIK). Established at the First All-Russian Congress of Soviets in early June 1917. After October 1917, the Congress of Soviets was formally the supreme organ of state power; between sessions, the VTsIK was.

Cheká, the All-Russian Extraordinary Commission for Combating Counterrevolution and Sabotage. Established 7 (20) December 1917 under Feliks Dzerzhinsky. Its role combined the fight against banditry, looting, and financial corruption with political police tasks. A network of provincial and district Chekas was established during 1918. The Cheka was the primary organ of the Red Terror during the civil war. It was succeeded by the GPU, the OGPU, and, in later years, the NKVD and the KGB.

Chemodúrov, Térenty Ivánovich (1849–1919). Valet to Nicholas II. Followed the imperial family into exile in Tobolsk and Yekaterinburg. In May 1918, because of illness, left the Ipatiev house and entered a local prison hospital. Freed by White soldiers on 25 July.

Council of People's Commissars (Sovnarkóm). Established on 26 October (8 November) 1917, chaired by Vladimir Lenin until his death in 1924. It was the executive and administrative branch of the Soviet government, the de facto dominant structure of state power.

Demídova, Anna Stepánovna (Niuta) (1878–1918). Alexandra's maid. Followed the imperial family into exile. Executed with the family on the night of 16–17 July 1918.

Den (Dehn), Yúlia Aleksándrovna (Lili) (b. 1880). An intimate of Alexandra's and Anna Vyrubova's. Took part in organizing communications between friends and sympathizers in Petrograd and the imperial family in Tobolsk.

Derevénko, Nikolái Vladímirovich (Kólia). Son of Doctor Vladimir Derevenko. One of tsarevich Aleksei's few regular playmates. Accompanied his father to Tobolsk and then Yekaterinburg.

Derevénko, Vladímir Nikoláevich (1879–1936). Distinguished court surgeon treating the tsarevich Aleksei from 1912. Followed the imperial family to Tobolsk and Yekaterinburg. The only person authorized to enter and leave the Ipatiev house in order to attend Aleksei.

Didkóvsky, Borís Vladímirovich (1883–1938). Bolshevik party activist and Beloborodov's deputy in the Ural Regional Soviet. Participated in the transfer of the imperial family from Tobolsk to Yekaterinburg.

Dolgorúkov (in some sources: Dologorúky), Vasíly Aleksándrovich (Vália) (1868–1918). Prince, major general in the imperial suite, marshal of the imperial court. Followed the tsar to Tobolsk. During the transfer of the imperial family from Tobolsk to Yekaterinburg, accused by Chekists of harboring weapons and plotting an escape. He was imprisoned and, together with Ilia Tatishchev, executed on 10 July 1918.

Elizabeth of Hesse-Darmstadt (Ella). See Yelizavéta Fyódorovna.

Frederíks, Emma Vladímirovna. Countess, daughter of the minister of the imperial court and domains Count Vladimir Borisovich Frederiks, lady-in-waiting to Alexandra. One of her frequent correspondents.

Géndrikova (Hendrikova), Anastasía Vasílievna (Nástenka, Nástinka). Countess, lady-in-waiting to Alexandra. Followed the imperial family into exile. Executed together with Yekaterina Shneider on the outskirts of Perm on 4 September 1918.

Germogén (Hermogen) (b. Geórgy Yefrémovich Dolganóv) (1858–1918). Bishop of Tobolsk and Siberia. Aided and ministered to the Romanovs during their exile in Tobolsk and was in contact with monarchists trying to organize their escape. Was arrested, held for ransom, and finally drowned in the Tura River by the Red Army along with other prisoners on 16 June 1918 as the Reds were fleeing Tobolsk.

Gibbs, Sidney (1876–1963). English instructor of Nicholas and Alexandra's daughters from 1908. Tutored Aleksei in English from 1913 to 1918. Went to Tobolsk with the imperial family; was separated from them in Yekaterinburg and sent to Tiumen; from there he returned to Tobolsk. He returned to Yekaterinburg in August 1918 to assist in the White investigation of the execution of the Romanovs.

Gilliard, Pierre (Zhílik) (1879–1962). Swiss citizen; tutor, French-language instructor, and governor to Aleksei. Followed the imperial family into exile in Tobolsk. During the transfer of the Romanovs to Yekaterinburg, was separated from them and sent to Tiumen. Married Aleksandra Teglyova in 1922.

Goloshchékin, Filípp Isáevich (1876–1941). Bolshevik from 1903; trained as a dentist; political exile. In late June and early July 1918, as a member of the Presidium of the Ural Regional Soviet Executive Committee, conducted negotiations with party and state leaders in Moscow on the fate of the imperial family.

Isa. See Buksgévden, Sofía Kárlovna.

Kharitónov, Iván Mikháilovich (1870–1918). Cook to the imperial family. Followed the Romanovs into exile in Tobolsk and Yekaterinburg. Executed with the family on the night of 16–17 July 1918.

Khitrovó, Margaríta Sergéevna (Rita) (1895–1952). Former lady-in-waiting to Alexandra, companion of Olga Nikolaevna's. Arrested for trying to join the imperial family in Tobolsk on her own initiative; accused of plotting a monarchist coup but released for lack of evidence.

Khokhriakóv, Pável Danílovich (1893–1918). Bolshevik from 1916. Closely associated with Yekaterinburg Bolsheviks in early 1918. Chairman of the Tobolsk Soviet from 9 April 1918.

After Nicholas, Alexandra, and Maria had left Tobolsk, he was in charge of transferring the remaining children and the rest of the Romanov suite from Tobolsk to Yekaterinburg.

Kobylínsky, Yevgény Stepánovich (1879–1927). Colonel, commander of the special purpose detachment guarding the imperial family from August 1917, and commandant of the Governor's House in Tobolsk, where they were imprisoned, until 2 May 1918. After the transfer of the family to Yekaterinburg, joined the White Army. Later married Klavdia Bitner.

Kólia. See Derevénko, Nikolái Vladímirovich.

Ksénia Aleksándrovna (Xénia) (1875–1960). Grand duchess, elder sister of Nicholas II; wife of Grand Duke Aleksandr Mikhailovich. After the February Revolution, lived as an exile in the Crimea together with her family and the dowager empress, Maria Fyodorovna.

Lénin, Vladímir Ilích (b. Ulyánov) (1870–1924). Communist revolutionary and ideologue, founder of the Bolshevik party and the Soviet state, chairman of the Council of People's Commissars (Sovnarkom) from 1917 to 1924, creator of Marxism-Leninism.

Lili. See Den, Yúlia Aleksándrovna.

Little One. See Aleksei Nikoláevich.

Liturgy of the Presanctified Gifts. Orthodox Liturgy celebrated on prescribed days during Great Lent and Passion Week, at which times the Eucharist is traditionally not consecrated on weekdays. Communion is distributed from reserved sacraments consecrated the previous Sunday. It includes both vespers and the obednitsa (see below).

María Fyódorovna (1847–1928). Born Princess Dagmar, daughter of King Christian IX of Denmark; married the future Alexander III in 1866. Mother of Nicholas II. After the February Revolution she lived as an exile in the Crimea together with her daughter Grand Duchess Ksenia Aleksandrovna and Ksenia's husband, Grand Duke Aleksandr Mikhailovich.

María Nikoláevna (Marie) (1899–1918). Grand duchess, third daughter of Nicholas and Alexandra. Executed together with her family in Yekaterinburg on the night of 16–17 July 1918.

Márkov, Sergéi Vladímirovich. Cornet in Alexandra's Crimean Cavalry Regiment, decorated for bravery. Sent to Tobolsk in fall 1917 by Petrograd monarchists and Anna Vyrubova to help organize the liberation of the imperial family. To this end he entered military service and commanded a Red Cavalry squadron in Tiumen. Arrested. After the Romanovs were transferred to Yekaterinburg he sought aid from the Germans in liberating the imperial family.

Mikhaíl Aleksándrovich (Mísha) (1878–1918). Grand duke, youngest brother of Nicholas II, heir to the throne from 1899 until the birth of Aleksei in 1904. On 3 (16) March 1917, the day after Nicholas abdicated in his favor, he declared that he would not assume the throne unless directed to do so by the Constituent Assembly. Exiled to Perm by the Council of People's Commissars (Sovnarkom) in March 1918. Abducted and executed by Chekists on the outskirts of Perm on the night of 12–13 June 1918.

Nagórny, Kleménty Grigórievich (1889–1918). Former sailor on the imperial yacht *Shtandart,* personal caretaker to Aleksei in Tobolsk and Yekaterinburg. Taken from the Ipatiev house together with Ivan Sednyov on 27 May 1918, arrested, and imprisoned. Both men were summarily executed by the Cheka in June 1918.

Narýshkina, Yelizavéta Alekséevna (Zizi) (b. 1840). Alexandra's grand mistress of the court, lady-in-waiting of the highest rank. Shared the imperial family's confinement in the Aleksandrovsky Palace in Tsarskoe Selo. One of Alexandra's frequent correspondents.

Nástenka, Nástinka. See Géndrikova, Anastasía Vasílievna.

Nicholas II. Civil name after abdication Nikolái Aleksándrovich Románov (1868–1918). Son of Alexander III and Maria Fyodorovna. Married Alix of Hesse-Darmstadt on 14 (26) November 1894. Succeeded to the Russian throne after the death of his father on 20 October (1 November) 1894. Crowned in Moscow on 14 (26) May 1896. Abdicated on 2 (15) March 1917 for himself and for his son, Aleksei, in favor of his brother Mikhail Aleksandrovich. Executed with his family in Yekaterinburg on the night of 16–17 July 1918.

Niúta. See Demídova, Anna Stepánovna.

Obédnitsa (diminutive of the Russian *obédnia,* "Liturgy"). A schematic celebration of the Liturgy, usually omitting the Eucharist, served by a priest when the full Liturgy cannot be celebrated due to lack of time or the necessary appointments, and also on "aliturgical days" (when the Eucharist is not consecrated). It may be read by the faithful when no priest is available.

Obolénskaia, Yelizavéta Nikoláevna (Lili). Princess and lady-in-waiting to Alexandra. One of her frequent correspondents.

Olga Aleksándrovna (1882–1960). Grand duchess and younger of the two sisters of Nicholas II. Her first marriage was to Prince Pyotr Aleksandrovich, the Duke of Oldenburg; her second, morganatic marriage in 1916 was to Colonel Nikolai Aleksandrovich Kulikovsky. In 1917 she gave birth to a son, Tikhon.

Olga Nikoláevna (1895–1918). Grand duchess, eldest daughter of Nicholas and Alexandra. Executed together with her family in Yekaterinburg on the night of 16–17 July 1918.

Pankrátov, Vasíly Semyónovich (1864–1925). Joined the Socialist Revolutionary Party in 1905. Appointed commissar in charge of the imperial family in Tobolsk by the Provisional Government in August 1917. Dismissed 26 January (8 February) 1918.

Rita. See Khitrovó, Margaríta Sergéevna.

Sednyóv, Iván Dmítrievich (1886–1918). Former crewman of the imperial yacht *Shtandart,* servant to Nicholas and Alexandra's daughters. Voluntarily shared the Romanovs' confinement in Tobolsk and Yekaterinburg; arrested on 27 May 1918 and executed together with Klementy Nagorny in June 1918.

Sednyóv, Leoníd Ivánovich (Lyónka) (b. 1904). Ivan Sednyov's nephew, apprentice cook, was with the Romanovs in Tobolsk and Yekaterinburg. On the eve of their execution he was removed by the Chekists, thereafter possibly sent to relatives in Kaluga Province.

Sergéi Aleksándrovich (Serge) (1857–1905). Grand duke, fifth son of Alexander II, uncle of Nicholas II. Married to Yelizaveta Fyodorovna (Ella), Alexandra's sister. Killed in Moscow by the Socialist Revolutionary terrorist Ivan Kaliaev.

Shnéider, Yekaterína Adólfovna (Trina) (1856–1918). Language tutor and lectrice to the imperial children. Followed the imperial family into exile. Accompanied the children from Tobolsk to Yekaterinburg, where she was arrested and imprisoned. Executed by Chekists along with Gendrikova and other prisoners on the outskirts of Perm on 4 September 1918.

Solovyóv, Borís Nikoláevich. Lieutenant, member of Rasputin's circle in Petrograd, in March 1917 an officer of the Military Commission of the State Duma Committee. In September 1917 married Rasputin's daughter, Maria (Matryona). Served as Anna Vyrubova's liaison between friends and sympathizers in Petrograd and the imperial family in Tobolsk, passing on money, gifts, and letters and plotting the Romanovs' escape. Arrested and soon released in March 1918.

Sovdép. Council of Workers', Peasants', and Red-Army Deputies. Early Soviet-period slang for "soviet," used by Alexandra in her diary to refer to the Omsk and Yekaterinburg Soviets.

Soviets. Councils of deputies elected by urban workers, peasants, and soldiers but also including representatives of leftist parties, trade unions, and other organizations. Ranged from neighborhood soviets in large cities like Moscow to regional soviets. First established during the 1905 revolution, they arose again in Petrograd in February 1917, then in most other Russian cities.

Sovnarkóm. See Council of People's Commissars.

Stórozhev, Fr. Ioánn Vladímirovich. Protopriest of St. Catherine's Cathedral in Yekaterinburg. With Deacon Buimirov, he twice served the obednitsa for the Romanovs in the Ipatiev house.

Sverdlóv, Yákov Mikháilovich (1885–1919). A leading figure in the Bolshevik party and Soviet state, directly in charge of the Romanov case. Bore direct responsibility for the fate of the Romanovs in Yekaterinburg and that of the other members of the imperial family executed in Alapaevsk the next night. The city of Yekaterinburg was renamed Sverdlovsk in his honor from 1924 to 1991.

Syroboiárskaia, María Martiánovna. Wife of artillery colonel Vladimir Syroboiarsky. Mother of Colonel Aleksandr Syroboiarsky. One of Alexandra's frequent correspondents.

Syroboiársky, Aleksándr Vladímirovich (1888–1946). An officer in the Russian army. During the civil war, he joined the anti-Bolshevik army of Admiral Kolchak.

Tatiána Nikoláevna (1897–1918). Grand duchess, second daughter of Nicholas and Alexandra. Executed together with her family in Yekaterinburg on the night of 16–17 July 1918.

Tatíshchev, Iliá Leonídovich (1859–1918). Count, adjutant general in the imperial suite, lieutenant general in the Guards Cavalry. Followed the imperial family to Tobolsk. Arrested after the transfer to Yekaterinburg (23 May 1918). Executed together with Valia Dolgorukov by the Cheka on 10 July 1918.

Teglyova, Aleksándra Aleksándrovna. Nanny to the imperial children. Shared their exile in Tobolsk and accompanied them to Yekaterinburg, where she was separated from them and sent to Tiumen. Married Pierre Gilliard in 1922.

Tolstáia, Zinaída Sergéevna (Zina, Zinochka). Wife of Colonel Pyotr Sergeevich Tolstoy of the Guards Cavalry. One of Alexandra's frequent correspondents.

Trina. See Shneider, Yekateri´na Adólfovna.

Trupp, Alekséi Yegórovich (1856–1918). Servant, followed the imperial family into exile in Tobolsk and Yekaterinburg. Executed with them on the night of 16–17 July 1918.

Vália. See Dolgorúkov, Vasíly Aleksándrovich.

Vladímir Nikoláevich. See Derevénko, Vladímir Nikoláevich.

Voéikova, Yevgénia Vladímirovna (Nini). Wife of court commandant Major General Vladimir Voeikov, lady-in-waiting to Alexandra. One of Alexandra's frequent correspondents.

Vóikov, Pyótr Lázarevich (1888–1927). Took part in supervising the confinement of the imperial family at the Ipatiev house, including drafting the four letters used in the abortive Cheka ploy to incite an escape attempt by the Romanovs. Participated in the execution of the Romanovs and the disposition of the corpses.

Vólkov, Alekséi Andréevich (b. 1859). Valet to Alexandra. Followed the Romanovs into exile; accompanied Olga, Tatiana, Anastasia, and Aleksei during their transfer from Tobolsk to Yekaterinburg, where he was separated from them and imprisoned in Perm. On the night of 4 September 1918, while being transferred under armed escort together with Gendrikova and Shneider to the site where the women were later executed, Volkov escaped.

VTsIK. See Central Executive Committee of Soviets of Workers', Peasants', and Red Army Deputies, All-Russian.

Vyrubova, Anna Aleksándrovna (Ania) (1884–1964). Lady-in-waiting and closest friend of Alexandra starting in 1904; acted as a go-between for Rasputin and the imperial family. In a train crash on 2 January 1915 she suffered a broken thigh and a serious spine injury. Doctors considered her case hopeless, but Rasputin was summoned, and Vyrubova and Alexandra believed that his supernatural powers saved Vyrubova's life (although she remained reliant on crutches). Arrested and imprisoned by the Provisional Government on 21 March 1917 on suspicion of aiding the Germans; released in June for lack of evidence. Provided assistance to the imperial family in Tobolsk and attempted to organize their escape.

Xénia. See Ksénia Aleksándrovna.

Yákovlev, Vasíly Vasílievich (Konstantín Alekséevich Miáchin) (1886–1938). Worked various factory jobs before turning full-time Bolshevik revolutionary, armed robber, and fighter, active mainly in the Urals. Among the first organizers of the Cheka. In the spring of 1918, the All-Russian Central Executive Committee (VTsIK) and the Council of People's Commissars named him extraordinary commissar in charge of transferring the imperial family from Tobolsk to Yekaterinburg. In this capacity he did everything possible—with Moscow's clearance—to protect Nicholas II from assassination attempts by Ural Red Guard detachments.

Yelizavéta Fyódorovna (Ella) (1864–1918). Grand duchess, born Elizabeth of Hesse-Darmstadt, sister of Alexandra, widow of Grand Duke Sergei Aleksandrovich. Became a nun. Arrested by the Cheka in April 1918 and deported first to Perm and then on 11 May to Yekaterinburg, where she was denied permission to visit the imperial family. Exiled with a number of Romanov princes to Alapaevsk (in the Urals) on 20 May 1918. Executed by the Cheka together with other members of the imperial family and others on the night of 17–18 July 1918.

Yevgény Sergéevich. See Bótkin, Yevgény Sergéevich.

Yuróvsky, Yákov Mikháilovich (1878–1938). Bolshevik from 1905. Appointed commandant of the House of Special Purpose (the Ipatiev house) on 4 July 1918 and entrusted with the imperial family's execution and the disposal of the bodies. Thereafter held high posts in the Cheka.

Yusúpov, Felíks Felíksovich (Felix, Count Sumarókov-Elston, the younger) (1887–1967). Prince. Married Princess Irina Aleksandrovna, Nicholas II's niece, in 1914. Participated in the murder of Grigory Rasputin in December 1916 with Vladimir Purishkevich (extreme rightist leader in the State Duma) and Grand Duke Dmitry Pavlovich; they believed they were saving the monarchy.

Zhílik. See Gilliard, Pierre.

Zina, Zínochka. See Tolstáia, Zinaída Sergéevna.

Zizi. See Narýshkina, Yelizavéta Alekséevna.

Sources Cited

Alfer'ev, Ye. Ye. *Imperator Nikolai II kak chelovek sil'noi voli* (Emperor Nicholas II as a man of strong will). Jordanville, N.Y.: Holy Trinity Monastery, 1983. Reprint, Moscow, 1991.

Avdeev, A. D. "Nikolai Romanov v Tobol'ske i Ekaterinburge" (Nicholas Romanov in Tobolsk and Yekaterinburg). *Krasnaia nov'* (Red virgin soil) 5 (1928).

Buxhoeveden [Buksgevden], Sophie. *The Life & Tragedy of Alexandra Feodorovna, Empress of Russia: A Biography.* London: Longmans, Green, 1928.

Bykov, P. M. *Poslednie dni Romanovykh* (The last days of the Romanovs). Sverdlovsk, 1926. Reprint, Sverdlovsk, 1990.

The Festal Menaion. Translated from the Greek by Mother Mary and Archimandrite Kallistos Ware. London: Faber & Faber, 1969.

GARF (State Archive of the Russian Federation). The citations in the notes use Russian abbreviations: op. (for subsection), f. (collection or catalog), d. (file or folder), and l. (page).

Gilliard, Pierre. *Thirteen Years at the Russian Court (A Personal Record of the Last Years and Death of the Czar Nicholas II and His Family).* Translated by F. Appleby Holt, O.B.E. 1921. Reprint, New York: Arno Press & The New York Times, 1970.

Iurovskii, Ia. M. "'Slishkom vse bylo iasno dlia naroda.' Ispoved' palacha" ("Everything was all too clear for the people": Confessions of an executioner). *Istochnik* (Source) 0 (1993).

Khrustalëv, V. M. "Taina 'missii' chrezvychainogo komissara

Iakovleva" (The secret of extraordinary commissar Yakovlev's "mission"). *Rossiiane* (Russians) 10 (1993).

Markov, Sergei. *Pokinutaia tsarskaia sem'ia, 1917–1918. Tsarskoe Selo—Tobol'sk—Ekaterinburg* (The forsaken imperial family, 1917–1918. Tsarskoe Selo—Tobolsk—Yekaterinburg). Vienna: 1928.

Mushits, Natal'ia. "Dnevniki Aleksandry Fedorovny Romanovoi kak istoricheskii istochnik" (The diaries of Alexandra Fyodorovna Romanova as a historical source). State Archive of the Russian Federation, 1997.

Nicholas II. *Dnevniki imperatora Nikolaia II* (The diaries of Emperor Nicholas II). Ed. K. F. Shatsillo. Moscow: Orbita, 1991.

Pipes, Richard. *The Russian Revolution.* New York: Random House, 1990.

Pis'ma tsarskoi sem'i iz zatocheniia (Letters from the imperial family in captivity). Ed. Ye. Ye. Alfer'ev. Jordanville, N.Y.: Holy Trinity Monastery, 1974.

Pokrovskii, Dmitrii. *Slovar' tserkovnykh terminov* (Dictionary of ecclesiastical terms). Moscow: RIPOL, 1995.

Radzinsky, Edvard. *The Last Tsar: The Life and Death of Nicholas II.* Translated by Marian Schwartz. New York: Doubleday, 1992.

Ross, Nikolai, ed. *Gibel' tsarskoi sem'i: Materialy sledstviia po delu ob ubiistve Tsarskoi sem'i (avgust 1918–fevral' 1920)* (The destruction of the imperial family: Investigatory materials on the murder of the Imperial family (August 1918–February 1920). Frankfurt: Possev, 1987.

Russkaia Letopis' (Russian chronicle). Vols. 1–4. Paris: "Russkii ochag," 1921–22.

Skorbnaia pamiatka (A mournful memento). Ed. A. V. Syroboiarskii. New York, 1928.

Sokolov, Nikolai. *Ubiistvo tsarskoi sem'i* (The murder of the imperial family). Berlin, 1925.

Steinberg, Mark D., and Vladimir M. Khrustalëv. *The Fall of the Romanovs: Political Dreams and Personal Struggles in a Time of Revolution.* New Haven: Yale University Press, 1995.

"Stenogrammy doprosov sledovatelem E. S. Kobylinskogo v kachestve svidetelia, a P. Medvedeva, F. Proskuriakova i A. Akimova v kachestve obviniaemykh po delu ob ubiistve imperatora Nikolaia II" (Transcripts of the investigator's interrogations of Ye. S. Kobylinsky as a witness, and P. Medvedev, F. Proskuriakov and I. Akimov as defendants in the murder of Emperor Nicholas II). *Istorik i sovremennik* (Historian and contemporary) (Berlin) 5 (1924).

Acknowledgments

Vladimir A. Kozlov and Vladimir M. Khrustalëv wish to express their gratitude to Z. I. Peregudova and P. I. Tiutiunik of the State Archive of the Russian Federation for their help with this volume. They especially wish to point out the large contribution to this publication made by Irene Burds and O. Lavynskaia (Poryvai), who went to great pains to decipher the 1917 and 1918 diaries.

Caryl Emerson provided valuable and generous advice concerning preparation of this text at an early stage. The editors would also like to thank Holy Transfiguration Monastery, Boston, for extensive assistance with biographical research and the treatment of liturgical terms; Father Michael Westerberg of Holy Transfiguration Orthodox Church, New Haven, for assistance with liturgical terms; and Marlene A. Eilers, for assistance with genealogical data. Richard Miller checked the diary transcription. We are grateful to Mark D. Steinberg and Vladimir M. Khrustalëv for permission to adapt the glossary and chronology that appeared in *The Fall of the Romanovs: Political Dreams and Personal Struggles in a Time of Revolution* (Yale University Press, 1995); Mark Steinberg also provided generous scholarly assistance during the final preparation of the notes.

ANNALS OF COMMUNISM

Each volume in the series Annals of Communism will publish selected and previously inaccessible documents from former Soviet state and party archives in the framework of a narrative text that focuses on a particular topic in the history of Soviet and international communism. Separate English and Russian editions will be prepared. Russian and American scholars work together to prepare the documents for each volume. Documents are chosen not for their support of any single interpretation but for their particular historical importance or their general value in deepening understanding and facilitating discussion. The volumes are designed to be useful to students, scholars, and interested general readers.